Ideal
Role Models

By
Shaykh Mufti Saiful Islām

JKN Publications

First Published in October 2017
ISBN: 978-1-909114-30-2

British Library Cataloguing in Publication Data
A catalogue record for this book is available from the British Library.

Publisher's Note:

Every care and attention has been put into the production of this book. If however, you find any errors they are our own, for which we seek Allāh's ﷻ forgiveness and the reader's pardon.

Published by:

JKN Publications
118 Manningham Lane
Bradford
West Yorkshire
BD8 7JF
United Kingdom

t: +44 (0) 1274 308 456 | w: www.jkn.org.uk | e: info@jkn.org.uk

Book Title: Ideal Role Models

Author: Shaykh Mufti Saiful Islām

Printed by Mega Printing in Turkey

"In the Name of Allāh, the Most Beneficent,
the Most Merciful"

Contents

4

Introduction

All Praises belong to Allāh ﷻ, the Lord of the worlds and may Peace and Blessings descend on His Final Messenger, Muhammad ﷺ, his Noble Companions, Family and those who follow their path until the Last Day.

As humans, we all aspire to emulate those who we look up to. Those who we consider as our role models, set a standard for us in how to live in the world. Many people aspire for wealth and fame in this world and sadly, this notion stems from watching famous pop stars and celebrities. As Muslims, we are here to please Allāh ﷻ and aspire for Jannah in the Hereafter and this is only possible if we attain piety and righteousness. To achieve this, we ought to read about the lives of our pious predecessors, their righteous conduct and way of living. Such people are true role models for us in this world. To succeed in both worlds, we must appreciate the fact that there are good and righteous people out there from who we can take benefit. Should we fail to learn from them and instead pursue the path of misguided people, then only we are to be blamed for our final destruction.

This book is a collection of articles from various social media avenues and bi-monthly Al-Mumin magazine, containing the lives and accounts of our pious predecessors. We hope our readers will benefit immensely from their lives and make a change in the way we behave and the way we think. I am grateful for Shaykh Mufti Saiful Islām

Sāhib for facilitating this project of compilation and to take benefit from him. I pray to Allāh ﷻ to preserve him and reward him immensely for his great services of Dīn, Āmīn.

Palwasha Ustarana, JKN Student

October 2017/Muharram 1439

A True Role Model

Have you ever heard of the famous Sahabi of the Holy Prophet ﷺ, Say-yiduna Anas Ibn Malik ؓ? He was the young boy who was the Khadim of the Holy Prophet ﷺ. He narrated many Ahadith from which we derive benefit to this day, including the famous Hadith about the beautiful character of our beloved Prophet ﷺ in which he said, "I served the Holy Prophet ﷺ for ten years and he never scolded me. Whatever I had done, he never asked me as to why I did that, or anything I had not done, he never asked me as to why I failed to do that." (Bukhari, Muslim)

Have you ever wondered how this great Sahabi became such a close Companion to our beloved Prophet ﷺ? Who was the driving force behind this illustrious character? Who paved the way for this man's success? It was none other than his amazing mother Sayyidah Umme Sulaym ؓ. She bravely sacrificed her young son by dedicating him to be in the personal service of the Holy Prophet ﷺ. How many of the women of today could be so selfless and brave as to give up their only child to the service of somebody else for even one day let alone ten years? We would probably have a difficult day without our child – who would nip to the shop for us to buy the milk or the bread? Who would throw out the bins for us? Or for some of us who would log us on to the internet or send for us a text message?! How would we cope?! It was due to the sheer devotion to the cause of Islam of this incredible woman that she and her son Anas ؓ were able to prosper so greatly and become so well known today for their great characters and services to Islam.

Sayyidah Umme Sulaym ؓ was one of the first women of Madinah Munawwarah to accept Islam. Her husband Malik did not accept Islam but this did not shake her strong faith or prevent her from inculcating the beautiful teachings of Islām to her beloved son Anas ﷺ. When her husband died, Sayyidah Umme Sulaym ﷺ devoted herself to the correct upbringing of Anas ﷺ with due care and consideration to her new religion, Islām despite the hardship involved in being a single parent.

News of her being widowed reached the ears of the strong and wealthy Sayyidunā Abū Talhah ﷺ. Though he was not a Muslim at that time he felt that his impressive qualities and the fact that he was from the same clan as Sayyidah Umme Sulaym ﷺ, would make it difficult for her to turn him down if he proposed to her. Furthermore, he had heard that her previous husband was not a Muslim so she would be unlikely to decline his offer just for this reason! So you can imagine Sayyidunā Abū Talhah's ﷺ surprise when he approached Sayyidah Umme Sulāym ﷺ to propose and she defiantly told him that though he was a very difficult man to turn down, she would never marry him as long as he was a disbeliever!

Look at the strength of this woman's character! The perfect man came knocking on her door at a time when she was a widowed single mum, but she was unwilling to compromise her faith for the temporary pleasures of this world. She would have been allowed to accept his proposal because the laws prohibiting a Muslimah from marrying a non-Muslim were not yet in place. How many of us women could confidently say we would do the same?

Furthermore, to add to the strength of Sayyidah Umme Sulaym's ﷺ character, she boldly added that if Sayyidunā Abū Talhah ﷺ wanted to marry her, she would accept as her dowry – not any of his riches or gold but his acceptance of Islām! Compare this with our women of today who demand a long list of worldly possessions from their husbands-to-be, leaving them struggling to attain the means to get married, not to mention vulnerable to sin.

Sayyidunā Abū Talhah ☬ thought deeply about Sayyidah Umme Sulaym's ﷺ proposition. His heart opened to the light of Īmān and he accepted her offer, declaring that there is no god but Allāh ﷻ and Muhammad ﷺ is the Messenger of Allāh ﷺ. The Muslims would say that they had never heard of a Mahr (dowry) more valuable than that of Sayyidah Umme Sulaym's ﷺ– Islām!

The couple devoted themselves to the cause of Islām and were of the blessed seventy-two who took part in the famous second Pledge of Aqabah, in which they took the oath of allegiance to the Holy Prophet ﷺ leading the way to his migration to Madīnah Munawwarah. Sayyidah Umme Sulaym ﷺ and Sayyidunā Abū Talhah ☬ lead exemplary lives as Muslims and their home was a place often visited by the Holy Prophet ﷺ.

With regard to Sayyidah Umme Sulaym's ﷺ role as a mother, we have already heard about her great sacrifices in relation to her first son Anas ☬. But her admirable character as a mother did not stop here. Sayyidah Umme Sulaym ﷺ and Sayyidunā Abū Talhah ☬ had a son whom they named Abū Umair. One day whilst Sayyidunā Abū Talhah ☬ was out working, the infant Abū Umair sadly passed away due to illness. Sayyidah Umme Sulaym ﷺ resolved to break the shattering news to her husband in a way which would limit the impact and pain as much as possible.

Sayyidunā Abū Talhah ☬ was fasting that day so after shrouding the body of her lost, beloved baby, she prepared food for her husband to break his fast. The couple then shared the bed for the night after which Sayyidah Umme Sulaym 🌸 asked her husband if somebody had entrusted him with their belongings, would he return it to them if they requested him to do so. Sayyidunā Abū Talhah 🌸 replied in the affirmative. Umm Sulaym 🌸 then told her husband that Abū Umair was entrusted to them by Allāh 🌸 but Allāh 🌸 had taken back that which belonged to Him.

Look at the beautiful patience of Sayyidah Umme Sulaym 🌸 and her pure faith in Allāh 🌸. If this had happened to any of us, I am sure we would have at least spent the day in complete sorrow and shock, if not been unable to control our tears throughout the day. But Sayyidah Umme Sulaym 🌸 was so strong that she could consider the feelings of others at such a testing time by ensuring that her husband had broken his fast and was comfortable and rested when she broke the distressing news to him. Furthermore, she did not despair or complain about her heart-breaking fate. Rather, she firmly understood that Allāh 🌸 has the right to do as He pleases with His slaves because in reality, our children belong to Him just as we all do and we should submit to His Will and have hope and trust in His Wisdom and Mercy. Allāh 🌸 demonstrated His Wisdom and Mercy by rewarding Sayyidah Umme Sulaym 🌸 for her incredible patience. He granted her another son from this night shared with her husband, through whom she had nine grandsons, all memorisers of the Holy Qur'ān!

Sayyidah Umme Sulaym 🌸 was a powerful woman of strength, courage, selflessness, passion, piety and devotion just to mention a few of her extraordinary qualities. Her faith and trust in Allāh 🌸 was beyond our imagination and the fruits of this were evident for us to see during many occasions in her life, as well as in the Hereafter, as confirmed by the Hadīth in which the Holy Prophet ﷺ mentions that he had been informed that Sayyidah Umme Sulaym ؓ was in Paradise.

What a heroic woman for us all to accept as a true role model. Unlike the women we perceive to be our role models today, who we usually admire merely for their beauty – something which was given to them by Allāh ﷻ that they never actually did anything admirable to achieve. If we take even a small glimpse into the personal lives of these people we would most probably no longer regard them as people to be admired. In comparison, women like Sayyidah Umme Sulaym ؓ possessed so much strength of character that we would be lucky if we could acquire even a fraction of it. May Allāh ﷻ give us the ability to recognise individuals like Sayyidah Umme Sulaym ؓ who are truly worthy of our admiration and emulation and to accept them as our true role models in life. Āmīn.

Shaykh Khalīl Sūfi Sāhib ﷺ

Shaykh Khalīl Sūfi Sāhib ﷺ was from Lajpore, India. Lajpore is a village of our Akābir and Mashā'ikh. He was from the Sūfi family and he truly was a Sūfi himself. After graduation, he first came to UK and then he travelled to Canada. He settled down in Toronto.

In the early 80s, there were hardly any Masājid in Toronto. Our respected teachers, Maulāna Hāshim Sāhib and Mufti Shabbīr Sāhib went there to lead Tarāwīh and deliver speeches. Towards the end of Ramadhān, they encouraged the community to purchase a property and start their own Masjid. (They had previously hired a hall for Tarāwīh.)

Mufti Shabbīr Sāhib delivered a lecture on the 27th night and collected funds. Ladies were so overwhelmed that many gave their jewellery. A property was bought on Danforth Avenue.

A committee was formed and Shaykh Khalīl Sāhib ﷺ was appointed as the young Imām, where he served tirelessly for over a quarter of a century and then remained their Amīr (leader) for the rest of his life.

He used to reside in Scarborough and travel from there by public transport. He would arrive in the morning and spend the whole day in the Masjid. Winter or Summer, snow or heat, the Shaykh would be in his office on time.

People would come with their queries and benefit from his clear cut answers. His Jumu'ah Khutbah (sermon) would be unique. People would travel from far and wide just to pray Jumu'ah behind him.

He was well versed with Dīni Masāil. When I was once in Masjid Nabawi in Madīnah Munawwarah for a few days of Ramadhān, we had a question and answer session. I had asked for written questions only. I sat down with Maulāna Marhūm and went through the questions. I noted down his answers and then added my own answers.

There was a question about smoking- whether it's Harām or Makrūh. I was of the opinion that it is Harām, as the Ulamā of Arabs have declared it Harām and many scholars also say this, based on the latest research on the harms of smoking. However, Maulāna Marhūm said, "To declare something Harām, you need a clear Nas Qat'ī (textual evidence) and there is no clear Nas for this." I took his view and replied to the congregation accordingly. I learned something new from him, may Allāh ﷻ elevate his ranks.

When the Mas'alah of degrees came to light, people were saying all sorts of things with regards to Ishā time and Suhūr time. I asked Shaykh Khalīl Sāhib ﷫ and he was very strong in his opinion. He said, "I have done extensive research on this. I have asked for Fatāwa from various places. Mufti Taqi Sāhib came here and I showed him all my research. He agreed with me. I also showed it to Mufti Rashīd Ahmad Ludhyānwi ﷫ and took his opinion on board. So, there is no reason why I should change."

Young scholars will come with new research, but I believe Shaykh Khalīl Sāhib ﷫ was the Imām Abū Hanīfah ﷫ of Toronto. His research was thorough and his piety was unquestionable. Ahlullāh (Friends of Allāh ﷻ) are inspired by Allāh ﷻ. He held the community together. His loss will be a huge loss to Toronto. As they say, 'Mawtul Ālim Mawtul Ālam' The death of a scholar is the death of the world.

One Hadīth says:

موت عالم مصيبة لا تُجبر و ثلمة لا تسد و موت قبيلة ايسر من موت عالم و هو نجم طمس (رواه الطبراني عن ابي الدرداء و روي نحوه الديلمي عن ابن عمر و البزار عن عائشة رضي الله عنهم)

"The death of an Ālim is an inconsolable calamity. It is a gap which cannot be filled. The death of a tribe is of less harm than the death of an Ālim. He was a star which has been erased." (Tabarāni)

Ulamā will come and go but Shaykh Khalīl Sāhib 🕮 will remain in our hearts forever. He always offered a warm welcome to his guests, especially the Ulamā. I can still recollect his arms wide open with a big hug and lots of Du'ās.

May Allāh 🕮 forgive Shaykh Khalīl Sāhib 🕮, elevate his ranks and give patience to his family and all connected. Āmīn!

(Shaykh Abdur Rahīm Sāhib, U.K)

The Red Diamond of South Africa

I was blessed with the opportunity to meet the erudite scholar, preacher, bastion of humility and jewel of South Africa, Shaykh Fadlur Rahmān A'zami (Hafidhahullāh).

In the past few years, I have travelled to South Africa on several occasions in order to conduct Hadīth programs and it was my desire to meet the world-renowned Muhaddith, but due to my heavy schedule or the Shaykh's travel plans, I was unable to meet him. However, I did speak to Shaykh on more than one occasion by phone, requesting his Du'ā for me to one day meet with him.

Then, recently after returning from the UK, I learnt from our dear brother Mufti Javed Iqbal of Birmingham, that Shaykhul Hadīth had arrived in the UK for Ramadhān and would be supervising a special Ulamā only Majlis for the auditory transmission of Imām Sunbul's 🕮 famous Hadīth collection. When I read his message, I felt gutted that once again I nar-

15

rowly missed the opportunity to meet the Shaykh and envied the good fortune of the UK Ulamā. I prayed that perhaps I could one day be blessed with such an opportunity of reading this work with the Shaykh as he had made some valuable corrections on the text and read it with the Grand Muhaddith, Shaykh Habībur Rahmān A'zami ﷺ who had also verified the text.

Unknown to me then and known to Allāh ﷻ, the prolific traveller Shaykh Fadlur Rahmān A'zami would a month later visit Malaysia for the first time in his life and by the will of Allāh ﷻ, I would also be in the same country.

A month later, when the Shaykh arrived in Malaysia, one of my students hosting him, called to inform me of his coming and that the program committee would like for me to attend. When I asked what text would be covered, he informed me that it would be Imām Sunbul's ﷺ Hadīth work. When he said this, I nearly fell off my chair in surprise that such an opportunity presented itself. I assured him I would happily attend and asked for the Shaykh's complete program.

Shaykh's program was in the South of the country at a distance of 300 plus kilometres from my home so it would take at least 6 hours to reach him. The Shaykh had a very busy schedule of mainly spiritual talks, some of which were private and others open to the public. I wanted to extract as much benefit as possible from the Shaykh, but I did not want to inconvenience his various hosts who also sought the same goal. Therefore, I decided to attend only the general talks in the hope that perhaps the Shaykh, on his own initiative, would intercede for my being allowed to spend more time in his company.

16

In the valuable moments of time that I shared with the esteemed Shaykh, I was able to glean great benefit in a variety of areas including his methodology in matters related to the science of Hadīth, his love for and adherence to the Sunnah, his time management, his immense humility, his generosity and kindness towards students of the sacred sciences, to name a few things.

Shaykhul Hadīth was informed by the hosts that I had been invited to attend his programme and that I was on the way. Sadly, the brother driving was not familiar with the route and we regularly lost our way, which meant we arrived after the conclusion of the Maghrib program and at the time Shaykh was making his way to eat.

After the long drive, I exited the car lethargically and the hosts came and asked me to rush as Shaykhul Hadīth requested my presence for supper. This kind gesture of the Shaykh was to set the tone for the high standard of Akhlāq (Islamic decorum) that I was to become accustomed to receiving from him in the short time I enjoyed his company.

I entered the room where the food had been placed, briskly greeted the Shaykh and sat down so as not to disturb him. Shaykh kept an eye on my plate and seeing that I was shy, requested the hosts to refill it on a few occasions.

After completing the food, Shaykh made the lengthiest 'after meal' Duā that I have heard. With complete fluency, he read all the variations of the authentic Masnūn Duās that were present in the books of Hadīth. This demonstrated to me his grasp of Hadīth and his regular practice of these supplications. This attention to detail in the observance of the Sunnah is commonly and incorrectly neglected by many teachers of the sacred sciences.

Despite, Shaykhul Hadīth's busy schedule that day and the late hour at which I arrived, he invited me to his sleeping quarters and I happily obliged. Shaykh then told me that he remembered a conversation I had with him a few years ago and that he was happy we were able to meet. I was touched that such a great scholar with all his concerns should even care to remember this feeble one.

Shaykhul Hadīth then mentioned the names of two of his South African students (Mufti Kadodia and Mufti Ibrāhīm) and asked if I knew them. After this, Shaykh asked me about my journey and the welfare of my family. We then discussed some issues pertinent to Hadīth, particularly whether he regarded the famous living Hadīth Muhaqqiqīn (manuscript editors) as Muhaddithīn. I listened to his definition and was pleased that my understanding was matched by someone of his stature.

As it was getting late, I requested some moments to read a few Ahādīth with the Shaykh and felt it best to seek his permission to leave as I could see that he was physically tired. He permitted me to leave providing that I would meet with him tomorrow. I informed him that I was with him until his flight back to South Africa the following night.

The following day at 10am, the Shaykh was scheduled to give a special talk for scholars in Malaysia. I attended the talk and found that the attendees numbered no more than 8 people. Where other scholars may have been demotivated by such a low attendance, Shaykh sincerely gave the teachers a passionate and lengthy session of Nasīhah and answered the questions posed to him at the end.

After the session, I went up to Shaykhul Hadīth to greet him and he invited me to join him for a snack. I accompanied him and the hosts into the apartment and sat on the ground with my children. Shaykh offered that I sit with him on the sofa to which I declined. Shaykh smiled and asked the hosts to bring some refreshments and snacks for us. The hosts brought a few things and placed them in front of us. Shaykh then went into the kitchen for some moments, opened the small fridge and with some effort, bent down to the fruit compartment and picked up some clear plastic bags of fruit. He then confirmed with the hosts if these were for him. They replied in the affirmative and he placed them on the floor in front of us and encouraged us to eat. Again, I was touched by the Shaykh's humility and generosity and his strict observance of the Sunnah by sharing his gifts with all those present with him.

It was then that I plucked up the courage to ask the Shaykh about my wife. I informed him that despite her ill-health, my wife had travelled with me over 300km in order to attend the planned al-Awā'il as-Sunbuliyah Majlis. If he permitted, she could attend his program. He asked about my wife's attire and history of study and I informed him that she wore the Khimār and had over the years travelled with me to study at the hands of scores of Ulamā around the world. He was impressed with her zeal and agreed to let her participate. I then left the Shaykh to take a noon siesta and informed him I would see him at the Majlis a few hours later.

About an hour later, I received a call from the host that Shaykhul Hadīth invited me to eat lunch with him after the prayer. Of course, I accepted the invitation as it meant I could enjoy precious moments with him again. I went to Shaykhul Hadīth and found that he was sitting on the floor waiting for me to join him before he started eating. I washed my hands and started eating with Shaykh. During the meal, Shaykh asked me some questions which brought up the Masnūn Du'ās for food. I told him that I would suffice with the brief formula that came in the Sunnah and re-frained from the practice of many in the subcontinent who say "Bismillāh wa 'alā Barakatillāh". I informed him that I never came across a Hadīth that stated this formula. He was very happy and said that he had made Tahqīq (research) on this very issue and agreed that he could not find it in any book of Hadīth, however he was able to find the wording, "Bismillāh Wa barakatillāh" in the collection of al-Hākim.

I then mentioned other commonly found practices that had no authentic proof and yet they were adopted by many, and found that in each Mas'a-lah (religious issue) I mentioned, the Shaykh had already studied the proofs and came to a similar conclusion. He lamented the fact that many scholars continued to imitate the traditions in their countries instead of following the authentic Masnūn supplications and Sunnah practices.

Frankly speaking, I was so excited to find someone who had such a simi-larity in their approach to virtually every issue that they found not in ac-cordance with the Sunnah and I was struck by the Shaykh's wonderful zeal for verifying positions that are traditionally held and more a product of incorrect custom than of following the Sunnah. This, I found to be tru-ly refreshing.

Later that day, I attended the Shaykh's Hadīth Majlis and there were too many benefits for me to recount in this short article. In essence, his sheer encyclopaedic knowledge of Hadīth, Fiqh and Qur'ān related subjects is simply amazing and I consider him to be one of the leading Muhaddithūn of our time, but then again where are the moles from the mountains?!

I encourage all students of Ilm (knowledge) in South Africa and world-wide to visit this blessed scholar and to seek his supplication and Suhbah (company), while he is still amongst us. Indeed, someone of his stature, deep insight, adherence to the Sunnah, equilibrium of thought and immense humility are as rare in today's world as a 10 carat red diamond is on this planet.

May Allāh ﷻ keep him amongst us for many more years. Āmīn!

(Shaykh Muhammad Daniel, Cordoba Academy)

When Shaykh Rashīd Ahmad Gangohi's 🕮 Vision Was Affected

Shaykh Rashīd Ahmad Gangohi's 🕮 vision was affected as the cataract lead to a decrease in vision. In todays society, the straight forward treatment for cataracts and its operation is available; however, this was not the case in those days.

The specialists made a request to Hadhrat. "Hadhrat, the treatment for the cataract can be operated and we are able to carry out the surgery."

The treatment could also be surgically carried out in those days.

Hadhrat replied, "What would the situation be for Salāh?"

The specialists replied, "You will be able to perform your Salāh; however, for certain days (one day, two days, three days – the time period was explained), you will not be able to make Sajdah (prostrate), so for that reason it is advisable to pray your Salāh with gestures."

After listening to this, Hadhrat responded, "What kind of Salāh are those that do not involve the Sajdah?"

For the remaining part of his life, Hadhrat tolerated the lack of vision. The cataract operation was not carried out strictly because of not being able to perform the Sajdah!

(Shaykhul Hadīth Hadhrat Maulāna Yūsuf Motāla Sāhib)

Amazing Moments of our Beloved Prophet ﷺ

How did Mu'ādh Ibn Jabāl ؓ feel when he heard the Messenger of Allāh ﷺ saying, "Mu'ādh, by Allāh, I most certainly love you?"

And how did Abdullāh Ibn Abbās ؓ feel when the Messenger of Allāh ﷺ embraced him and said, "O Allāh, teach him the Book?"

Or how did Ali Ibn Abī Tālib ؓ feel when he heard the Messenger of Allāh ﷺ saying, "Tomorrow, I will definitely hand the banner to a man who loves Allāh ﷻ and His Messenger ﷺ, and whom Allāh ﷻ and His Messenger ﷺ also love," and then he found out that he was the one?

What was Sa'd Ibn Abī Waqqās's ؓ feeling when the Messenger of Allāh ﷺ said to him, "Throw it, Sa'd, may my parents be ransomed for you?"

And how did Uthmān Ibn Affān ؓ feel when he fully supplied the army heading to Tabūk and the Messenger of Allāh ﷺ said, "Nothing 'Uthmān ؓ does after today could ever harm him?"

Or how must Abū Mūsa Al-Ash'ari ؓ have felt when the Messenger of Allāh ﷺ said, "If you could have only seen me while I was listening to your recitation yesterday?"

And how did Sā'ib Ibn Yazīd ؓ feel when only the patch of hair that the Messenger of Allāh ﷺ wiped on his head remained black whilst the remainder of his hair turned white due to old age?

And what emotions did the Ansār experience when the Messenger of Allāh 📖 said to them, "If all people were to go one way and the Ansār were to take another, I would choose the path of the Ansār."

And how did the Ansār feel when the Prophet of Allāh 📖 spoke about them saying, "The sign of belief is love for the Ansār, and the sign of hypocrisy is feeling animosity toward them."

And what were the feelings of Abū Bakr Siddīq 📖 when the Messenger of Allāh 📖 said, "If I were to take a bosom friend, I would have taken Abū Bakr as my bosom friend?"

How did Sayyidah Āisha 📖 feel when the Messenger of Allāh 📖 replied unhesitatingly with her name when he was asked who was the most beloved person to him?

And what were the feelings of Bilāl Ibn Rabāh 📖 when Allāh's Messenger 📖 said to him, "O' Bilāl, tell me about the deed in which you place most hope, for I have heard the striking of your shoes in front of me in Jannah?"

And how did Umar Ibn Khattāb 📖 feel when he sought permission to enter upon the Messenger of Allāh 📖 and he told the doorman, "Allow him to enter and give him glad tidings of Paradise?"

How did all the Sahābah 📖 feel while seeing the Messenger 📖 morning and evening?

And how are we going to feel when we see the Messenger of Allāh 📖, and he says to us, "You are my brothers for whom I have cried in my anticipation to meet; you are my brothers who have believed in me without ever seeing me?"

O' Allāh ﷻ, make us from amongst them. Āmīn.

Interesting Incident of Mufti Mahmūdul Hasan Gangohi ﷫

Hadhrat Mufti Sāhib ﷫ was very quick witted. Once, a pundit who occasionally paid him a visit asked the following question:

Pundit: Mufti Sāhib, there's a very strange Mas'alah in your religion.

Mufti Sāhib: We're all strange and unique. Tell me what additional thing have you discovered?

Pundit: There are two animals that are similar in shape and form, but one is Halāl and the other is Harām. The goat is Halāl and the pig is Harām. What's the reason for this?

Mufti Sāhib: Pundit Jee! My answer will be bitter for you to swallow, so please don't become angry.

Pundit: The answer can't be so terrible.

Mufti Sāhib: The answer is such that, the hair in your nose will burn, the skin on your face to your neck will peel away and you will never ask this question ever again. However, I shall try to explain it in such a manner that will hopefully be acceptable to you. Listen carefully.

Who will we refer to as a blind person? It's obvious that one who equates the goat and the pig, in respect to shape and size, is blind. (Pointing to himself) A goat has a beard whereas (pointing to the pundit) a pig doesn't have one. A goat eats fodder and grass whilst a pig eats faeces and filth. A goat (ewe) has two udders whilst a pig has more. A goat has horns and a pig doesn't. In short, both have different shapes and even the formation of their limbs are different.

Nevertheless, we accept that there are some blind people (who cannot differentiate between them) and we must consider them. Very well, tell me, is your mother alive?

Pundit: Yes.

Mufti Sāhib: Do you have a sister?

Pundit: Yes.

Mufti Sāhib: Do you have a wife?

Pundit: Yes.

Mufti Sāhib: Do you also have children?

Pundit: Yes, I have two children.

Mufti Sāhib: From whom were these children born?

Pundit: What do you mean 'from whom'?

Mufti Sāhib: There are three women in your home, your mother, sister and wife. Which of these women bore your children?

At this question, the pundit became enraged.

Pundit: My children are from my wife. From whom else can they be?

Mufti Sāhib: Your mother, sister and wife are all women. Their forms and appearances are the same. Each of them have two eyes, two ears and two feet. However, why do you then regard your wife as Halāl (permissible) and your mother as Harām (unlawful)? If there is an age gap between your mother and wife then there's no real difference between your wife and sister. So why do you consider your wife as lawful and sister as unlawful?

The pundit replied in a fit of rage.

Pundit: This is the level of a Muslim's character. You pick on the mothers and sisters of others!

Mufti Sāhib: May Allāh ﷻ forgive us. Pundit Jee, you've misunderstood me. I'm not picking on your mother or sister. If this is what you have understood, then I don't blame you for becoming angry. A noble person will definitely be enraged if someone picks on his mother and sister. (You were the one who commenced by saying that both animals are the same, but Islām is a very strange religion, since it allows the consumption of one and forbids the other.)

The pundit then began to speak in an irrational manner.

Mufti Sāhib: I had initially stated that the answer will be bitter for you to swallow but I had removed some of the bitterness.

Pundit: Why don't you say those bitter words as well!

Mufti Sāhib: Must I really say it?

Pundit: Yes.

Mufti Sāhib: It seems that you've acquired some level of tolerance. So listen carefully. There is no difference between the two of us. Then why do you regard your wife as lawful for yourself and not for me? Similarly, there's no difference between your brother-in-law and myself, but why is it that your sister is lawful for him and not for me. In the same vein, why do you consider your mother as lawful for your father and not for me whereas there's no difference between your father and me? In fact, if his attire is similar to the people of the past, then perhaps he might have a beard as well. In short, both of us are the same, but why is your mother lawful for him and not for me?

The Pundit became incensed and blurted all the expletives he had in his vocabulary! (Malfūzāt Faqīhul-Ummah)

Shaykh Yahyā Sāhib 🌸 Invites Shaykh Thānwi 🌸 to the Nikāh of his Younger Brother

Shaykh Yahyā Sāhib 🌸, the father of Shaykhul-Hadīth, Shaykh Zakariyya Sāhib 🌸 had arranged the Nikāh of Shaykh Muhammad Ilyās Sāhib 🌸. He invited four pious scholars to the Nikāh; Shaykh Abdur Rahīm Sāhib Raipūri 🌸, Shaykhul-Hind Shaykh Mahmūdul Hasan Sāhib 🌸, Shaykh Khalīl Ahmad Sahāranpūrī 🌸 and Shaykh Ashraf Ali Thānwi 🌸. The first three saints accepted the invitation, but Shaykh Thānwi 🌸 did not accept it.

Shaykh Yahyā Sāhib 🌸 made arrangements for these pious elders to take the night train from Sahāranpur and meet him at Thānā Bhawan station. He took the morning train and went to meet Shaykh Thānwi 🌸. As he met him, he said, "Jī ha, your Taqwā has surpassed the Taqwā of your teacher, Shaykhul-Hind 🌸. It has also surpassed that of Shaykh Abdur Rahim Sāhib 🌸 and Shaykh Sahāranpūrī 🌸. They have accepted, but you have not accepted."

Shaykh Thānwi 🌸 replied, "Nowadays, there are many customs prevalent in weddings and therefore I stay away from attending wedding functions." Shaykh Yahyā Sāhib 🌸 then said to him, "It is for this reason that we are taking you along. If you see anything wrong, you should stop it immediately. Otherwise, what relations do I have with you that I must invite you to the wedding? I am taking you especially to stop all these customary practices."

Shaykh Thānwi ﷺ finally accepted the invitation. In the evening Shaykh Yahyā Sāhib took Shaykh Thānwi ﷺ along to the station and met the other three pious elders. (Malfūzāt of Faqīhul-Ummah Vol.2)

Shaykh Husain Ahmad Madani ﷺ
Honouring his Guest

Maulāna Shamsul Haq Afghāni ﷺ once mentioned while addressing the Ulamā: "I had once travelled to Deoband where I stayed as a guest of Shaykh Husain Ahmad Madani ﷺ. At the time of my arrival Shaykh was not present; hence I went to bed before he returned. In the middle of the night, my eyes opened to find that Shaykh Madani ﷺ was lying beside my bed on a straw mat with a brick under his head. I was totally ashamed and asked, 'Hadhrat! What is the matter? Why are you sleeping on the floor? Couldn't you get me up?' Shaykh Madani ﷺ replied, 'This is a gesture of Ikrāmud-Dhayf (honouring the guest). Haven't you read the Hadīth: "Whoever believes in Allāh ﷻ and the Hereafter should honour his guest?"

On this journey, I had also brought along a large quantity of grapes from Quetta. On receiving it, Shaykh Madani ﷺ distributed it to all those present. The attendant had then come from inside his home and requested, 'Maulāna Afghāni has brought along some grapes; pass over some for the house.' Hadhrat ﷺ replied, 'You have only come now. It has all been distributed.'

When it was time for meals, Hadhrat ﷺ lifted the water jug to wash the hands of those present. I told him, 'Hadhrat! What are you doing? I can wash my hands by myself.' However, Shaykh Madani ﷺ insisted on pouring the water. I then told him, 'What is the benefit in this argument? My heart has now been burdened. Is this Ikrāmud-Dhayf (honouring the guest)? Ikrāmud-Dhayf means that the guest should not undergo any type of difficulty.' Shaykh Madani ﷺ replied, 'You may experience some difficulty in fulfilling the injunction of Sharī'ah but Ikrāmud-Dhayf is also a command of Sharī'ah which I will fulfil.'" (Khutubāt-e-Akābir, Vol. 2)

Condoning the Wrong in a Wedding

Once, Shaykh Khalīl Ahmad Sahāranpūrī ﷺ was invited to a wedding in Meerut. The groom's side requested Hadhrat ﷺ to pass on the clothing to the groom for Tabarruk (blessing). Hadhrat ﷺ went into the room where the groom was waiting after having had a bath. I (Mufti Āshiq Ilāhi) was present with Hadhrat ﷺ. He picked up the Kurta (shirt) and pants and handed these over to the groom. When he was about to pass the Achkan (long coat), Hadhrat ﷺ asked me to check if it was made of silk. I checked carefully and said: "Yes Hadhrat ﷺ, it appears to be of silk." He kept it aside and said: "It is Harām to wear silk and Harām to make others wear it." When he looked at the topi, he saw it embedded with gold threads and so he said in a sharp tone: "This is also Harām." The groom's family was not cautious and did not bother about Hadhrat's ﷺ reprimand.

They picked up the items themselves and made the groom wear them. Hadhrat's ﷺ face turned red with anger but he controlled himself and said to me: "Let's go," and we departed from there. He did not even go to the place where he was staying over. He was filled with sorrow and grief, so he went to the house of Hāji Wajīhud Dīn Sāhib. He said: "What type of bond do they have with me that they invite me to take part in sinful acts? All those who attend this wedding will be sinning, for it is a place where the bridegroom is seated wearing Harām clothing, as one person (the bridegroom) will be committing the Harām and there will be others (the attendees) who will condone it."

When the family heard of this, they felt ashamed because it was an issue of family pride. Many people were attached to Hadhrat ﷺ – they could neither leave him nor leave the family. They tried to get the groom to change his clothes. However, many of the people had neither any attachment to Hadhrat ﷺ nor any concern for following the Shari'ah. They considered the changing of clothes to be an ill-omen and said: "It is essential for the bridegroom to wear the clothes which have been sent to him from the bride's family." However, the others were sharper than them. Hāji Wajīhud Dīn Sāhib took out his expensive Egyptian Achkan (long coat) and gave it to the groom saying he will not get a better suit than this in the whole of India. He made him wear it, and instead of the topi, he tied a turban on his head. He presented the groom before Hadhrat ﷺ and requested him to attend the wedding. Hadhrat ﷺ got up and joined in the wedding. (Tazkiratul Khalīl, pg. 322)

Sound Advice from Sayyidunā Umar ⬥

Sayyidunā Umar ⬥ said, "Take account of your own selves (i.e. of your deeds) before you will be taken to account (on the Day of Resurrection). Weigh yourselves (i.e. your deeds) before you will be weighted (i.e. before your deeds will be put on the balances on the Day of Resurrection).
Verily, if you hold yourselves accountable today, the accountability tomorrow (i.e. the Day of Resurrection) will be easier upon you. And adorn yourselves for the greater display (i.e. for when you will be brought to Judgement).

$$يَوْمَئِذٍ تُعْرَضُونَ لَا تَخْفَى مِنْكُمْ خَافِيَةٌ$$
"That Day you will be brought to Judgement, not a secret of you will be hidden." (69:18)

Sayyidunā Umar ⬥ once said to Ahnaf Ibn Qais ⬥, "O' Ahnaf, the more one laughs, the less dignity he will possess. Whoever jokes (excessively or indecently) is a person who will be taken lightly. Whoever does something frequently will become known by that thing. Whoever speaks often, errs often; the more often one errs, the less modesty will he possess; whoever has a low level of modesty will also have a low level of piety; and when one has a low level of piety, then his heart dies."

When advising an individual, Sayyidunā Umar ⬥ said, "Do not speak about that which does not concern you. Know your enemy and be wary of your friend, except for the trustworthy one; and no one is trustworthy except for the person who fears Allāh ⬥. Do not walk with the evil doer, lest he teaches you some of his wickedness and do not reveal your secrets to him. When you consult others in your affairs, consult only those who fear Allāh ⬥."

Sayyidunā Julaybīb 羲

It is narrated in the books of history that Sayyidunā Julaybīb 羲 was a Sa-hābi who was short in height and deformed in appearance. His lineage was not known. No one knew who his parents had been. With no clan to protect him and no tribe willing to accept him as their own, he was a lonely figure and even the small children of Madīnah Munawwarah would tease and mock him. Owing to his disabilities, no one would allow him to sit in their company. He survived as best as he could.

Many a lonely night in Madīnah Munawwarah he spent wondering the streets in despair. Tears of desperation would run down his cheeks. There was no one willing to offer him love or compassion. He had no family and not a single friend in the world. Life for him was a lonely struggle.

After the arrival of the Holy Prophet 羲 to Madīnah Munawwarah, the fortunes of Sayyidunā Julaybīb 羲 changed. He would go and sit in the company of the Holy Prophet 羲 and listen intently, rarely speaking. Out of shyness, he would keep his gaze lowered. Now he had the best of friends in the Holy Prophet 羲. Those days of loneliness and despair were over, for the best of Creation 羲 had arrived. Sayyidunā Julaybīb 羲 was now part of the community of believers.

One day, as he was sitting in the company of the Holy Prophet 羲, the Holy Prophet 羲 asked him. "O' Julaybīb! Ask for something! Is there anything you desire?" He raised his head slowly and said in a shy voice, "O' Messenger of Allāh 羲, Allāh 羲 has blessed me with your companionship. I get to sit at your blessed feet and hear your blessed words. What more could I desire?" The Holy Prophet 🌸 asked, "How would you like to get married, my dear Julaybīb?" He smiled shyly, wondering who would want to marry him, "Yes, O' Messenger of Allāh 🌸 I would like that."

The Holy Prophet 🌸 went to the house of a prominent and noble Sahābi from amongst the Ansār. He said, "I have come to ask for your daughter's hand in marriage." The Sahābi was overjoyed. He said, "O' Messenger of Allāh 🌸, what could be a greater blessing than this?" The Holy Prophet 🌸 said, "I do not ask of her for myself. It is for Julaybīb that I am asking." The Sahābi was left stunned. "For Julaybīb?" he asked in bewilderment. "Yes, for Julaybīb," replied the Holy Prophet 🌸.

He said, "Let me consult with my wife." He went and told her, "The Messenger of Allāh 🌸 has asked for your daughter's hand in marriage for Julaybīb." She started crying and wailing, "No, not Julaybīb! Anyone but Julaybīb! I will never allow this!" Upon hearing the commotion, the daughter arrived. It is said that she was so beautiful that there was none among the women of the Ansār who could compete with her looks. She was so shy and modest that perhaps the sky itself had never seen her head uncovered. She had so much Taqwā that she would spend her days and nights in worship.

As the mother continued her crying and wailing, the daughter said, "O' my mother, leave our own decision once Allāh 🌸 and His Messenger 🌸 have decided on a matter. Do you think that the Messenger of Allāh 🌸 will disgrace us? How blessed is the status of Julaybīb, that Allāh 🌸 and His Messenger 🌸 are asking for your daughter's hand on his behalf? Don't you know that the angels themselves envy the dust on the feet of one who is a beloved of Allāh ﷻ and His Messenger ﷺ? Ask the Holy Prophet ﷺ to send me Julaybīb for there is no greater privilege than for me to be blessed by such a husband. The Holy Prophet ﷺ has arrived with such a wonderful gift, yet my mother, you cry and wail."

The mother's heart being filled with remorse said, "Stop my daughter. Don't say another word. Indeed I have erred, I repent and I repent a thousand times over, for as of this moment, there is no one who I would prefer for you than Julaybīb."

Marriage

The following day the Nikāh was performed. Sayyidunā Uthmān ﷺ and Sayyidunā Ali ﷺ presented Sayyidunā Julaybīb ﷺ a gift of money to help arrange the feast of the Walīmah. A short time later, on an expedition, Sayyidunā Julaybīb ﷺ was martyred. On the day of the expedition, his father-in-law had pleaded with him, "O' Julaybīb, this is just an expedition. It is not a compulsory Jihād, it is Fardh-e-Kifāyah; it is a voluntary Jihād. As you are newly married spend some time with your wife."

Sayyidunā Julaybīb ﷺ, the one who had spent a lifetime in despair had now found a loving wife. However, listen to his response to his father-in-law's request. He said, "O' my father, you say a strange thing. My beloved Prophet ﷺ is in the battlefield facing the enemies of Islām and you want me to sit at home with my wife? Nay, I will sacrifice my blood and my soul rather than see my beloved Prophet's ﷺ hardship while I sit at home in luxury!"

Martyrdom

The diminutive Sayyidunā Julaybīb ﷺ was indeed a strange sight carrying a sword almost the same size as him. The Sahābah ﷺ stared in wonderment at him. The sweet and gentle Julaybīb was transformed into a lion. "Who dare wage war upon my beloved Prophet ﷺ?" he said, as he charged into the ranks of the enemy. After that battle, the Holy Prophet ﷺ asked the Sahābah ﷺ to go and see if anyone was missing from their families and clans. Each one returned accounting for all his family members.

The Holy Prophet's ﷺ Tears

The Holy Prophet ﷺ spoke with tears in his eyes and said, "But I have lost my beloved Julaybīb. Go and find him." They found his diminutive body lying next to seven enemies he had slain in the battle. The Holy Prophet ﷺ asked for a grave to be dug. As the Holy Prophet ﷺ held the body of Julaybīb, he said, "O' Allāh ﷻ, he is from me and I am from him." He repeated this three times. The Companions ﷺ wept profusely, "May our mothers and fathers be sacrificed for you, O' Julaybīb, how great is your status."

Thus, a Sahābi who had once lived as an outcast, was shunned by the society around him. He loved Allāh ﷻ and His Messenger ﷺ and reached such a high status. He who was not good looking was blessed with a beautiful wife. He who was poor was blessed by a wealthy wife. He who had no family or status was blessed by a wife with noble status and lineage. **He who had lived in loneliness and despair was loved by Allāh ﷻ and His Messenger ﷺ.** He had the Messenger of Allāh ﷺ stating, "O' Allāh ﷻ, he is from me and I am from him."

It is said that upon his martyrdom, the sky itself was filled with thousands of angels who had come to participate in his funeral prayers. Sayyidunā Julaybīb ⚬, 'the lonesome one' had become a beloved of Allāh 🟤 and His Messenger ⚬. He was lonely no more.

Mālik Ibn Dīnār 🟤

It was a dark night on which the burglar scaled the wall of Mālik Ibn Dīnār's 🟤 house and stealthily made his way inside. To his utter disappointment, the thief found nothing in the house that was worth stealing. What's more, the occupant of the house was actually inside and was busy praying.

Mālik Ibn Dīnār 🟤 sensed the movement of the burglar, but without becoming alarmed, he turned around with perfect composure and extended greetings of peace to him. He then said, "My brother, may Allāh 🟤 forgive you. You entered my home and found nothing worth taking, but I will not allow you to leave without gaining some benefit."

Mālik Ibn Dīnār 🟤 stood up, approached the burglar with a jug of water in his hands and said, "Here, perform ablution and perform two units of prayer. If you do so, you will take away with you that which is better than what you came to find in the first place."

"Yes, how generous of you," said the burglar, somewhat amazed and more than anything else, humbled. He stood, made ablution and performed two units of prayer. Upon completing them, he turned and said, "O

Mālik, will I be imposing upon you if I perform two more units of prayer?" "Perform as much as Allāh ﷻ decrees for you," said Mālik Ibn Dīnār ﷺ. The burglar turned worshipper continued to pray until the morning, at which time Mālik Ibn Dīnār ﷺ said, "Go and be good."

"Will I be imposing upon you if I stay here with you today, for I have made the intention to fast?"

"Stay as long as you want," said Mālik Ibn Dīnār ﷺ. The man stayed with Mālik Ibn Dīnār ﷺ for a number of days, spending the days fasting and the nights standing up for prayer. Finally deciding to leave, the man said, "O Mālik, I have made up my mind to repent."

"That (i.e. Allāh ﷻ forgiving you and guiding you to repent) is in the Hands of Allāh ﷻ," said Mālik Ibn Dīnār ﷺ. In fact, the man did mend his ways and repented from his previous sins. When the man left Mālik Ibn Dīnār's ﷺ home, he came across another burglar he knew. Seeing the happy and serene expression on the man's face, the other burglar said, "I think you have finally found your treasure?"

"My brother," he answered, "I found Mālik Ibn Dīnār. **I went to steal from him, but it was he who stole something of mine - my heart.** Indeed I have repented to Allāh ﷻ and I will remain at the door (of His Mercy and Forgiveness) until I achieve what His obedient, loving slaves have achieved."

The Change

Hind was the wife of Abū Sufyān, a chief of Makkah. In the early days of Islām, she was against the Holy Prophet 🕌 and the Muslims. She would do everything in her power to attack and hurt the Muslims. She was so against Islām that she would even accompany the Makkan army to fight against the Muslims. She would beat drums and sing songs which encouraged the men to fight harder against the poor Muslims. She hired the slave, Wahshi, who was a master javelin thrower, to track down Sayyidunā Hamzah 🕊, the Holy Prophet's 🕌 uncle. She told him to kill Sayyidunā Hamzah 🕊 and in return she would free him and also make him very rich. When Wahshi carried out this evil act, she went and cut off the ears and nose of Sayyidunā Hamzah 🕊 and made a necklace from it. She had much bitterness and hatred inside for the Holy Prophet 🕌 and the Muslims. She had spent most of her life in this evil state and everyone knew of her bad behaviour towards the Muslims.

When the Holy Prophet 🕌 returned to Makkah after many years, all of Makkah accepted the Holy Prophet 🕌 into their city. They were terrified, especially Hind, that the Holy Prophet 🕌 would take his revenge because of their cruelty in the past. The Holy Prophet 🕌 forgave all the Makkans and Hind began to see the Holy Prophet 🕌 in his true light. As she spent a little time with the Holy Prophet 🕌, she became influenced by his wonderful character and became a Muslim. This was after spending only a short time in Holy Prophet's 🕌 good company.

Al-Miski 🐝 (The One Who Emitted a Good Odour)

It is reported that Abū Bakr Al-Miski 🐝 was once asked, "We always find a good odour emanating from you; why or how?

He answered, "By Allāh 🕌, for years now I have not used any perfume. The reason for the good smell has to do with an ordeal that I passed through. A woman once tricked me into entering her home. Then she closed (and locked) the door behind her, after which she began to seduce me. I became utterly bewildered as to what I should do, for I had no options before me. I said to her, 'I need to go and purify myself.' She ordered her servant to take me to the bathroom and when I entered it, I took faeces in my hand and wiped it all over my body. Then I returned to her in that state. Shocked to see me like that, the woman ordered that I be removed from her home. I left and immediately took a shower.

That very night I saw a dream; in it, it was said to me, 'You have done that which no one else has ever done. I will make your smell good and pure in this world and in the Hereafter.' When I woke up, the smell of perfume was emanating from my body and it has continued to emanate from my body until this very moment."

Fragrance from a Grave

A group of learned scholars were travelling through some villages in Pakistan. They reached a particular city when some people approached them and asked them to visit a particular graveyard. Upon reaching the graveyard, they smelt a beautiful fragrance coming out of the newly dug grave. The villagers asked the scholars if they knew why this smell was emanating from that particular grave. The scholars decided to meet some family members of that person who died to find out what he used to do. After meeting them, they discovered that the man did not know how to recite the Holy Qur'ān. However, after every Fajr Salāh, he would sit with the Holy Qur'ān and put his fingers on the verses and say, "My Lord has spoken the truth here. My Lord has spoken the truth here." The scholars concluded that this was the reason why a beautiful fragrance was coming from the man's grave, due to his deeds.

Sayyidunā Umar's ﷺ Letter to the River Nile

After Egypt was conquered by the Muslims, the newly appointed Governor of Egypt, Sayyidunā Amr Ibnul Ās ﷺ one day held an open discussion in his court. Someone told him, "O Leader! During the ancient times, there was a custom which the locals practiced that kept the River Nile flowing. On the 11th day of every lunar month, we would take a young girl, with the consent of her parents, adorn her with the best of clothes and finest jewellery and sacrifice her to the River Nile."

When he heard this, Sayyidunā Amr Ibnul Ās ﷺ objected that this practice is most certainly not acceptable or permissible in Islām. Islām has come to remove such barbaric and evil customs. That year, this custom was abandoned and it so happened that the River Nile started drying out. Many people were forced to abandon their homes and migrate.

Sayyidunā Amr Ibnul Ās ؓ narrated this entire episode by letter to Amīrul Mu'minīn, Sayyidunā Umar ؓ.

Sayyidunā Umar ؓ wrote back that indeed Islām has come to destroy such evil customs. Together with the reply, he wrote another letter, which he said should be thrown into the River Nile. The Governor read out this letter, which contained the following,

"From the servant of Allāh ﷻ Umar, Amīrul Mu'minīn to the River Nile. If you flow on your own accord, then do not flow, but if Allāh ﷻ, The One and Mighty, makes you flow, then we beseech Allāh ﷻ, The One and Mighty to make you flow."

The Governor of Egypt threw this letter into the River Nile and the next morning when the people awoke, they saw that during the course of one night, Allāh ﷻ had made the River Nile rise by more than 100 hand-lengths. In this way, Sayyidunā Umar ؓ put an end to the evil custom of girl sacrifice. The greatness of Allāh ﷻ also manifested that ever since that time, the River Nile has continued flowing.

It is indeed true that whoever becomes Allāh's ﷻ, Allāh ﷻ becomes his. When Allāh ﷻ becomes his, then all the creation of Allāh ﷻ obey his instructions. The Sahābah ؓ had sacrificed everything of theirs for Allāh ﷻ. Hence, Allāh ﷻ had made the entire creation subservient to them. We should endeavour to follow the footsteps of the Sahābah ؓ in our daily lives.

Waking Up a Sleeping Person for Salāh

It is correct to wake up a sleeping person for Salāh. Once, the Holy Prophet ﷺ had seen someone sleeping in the Masjid and instructed a Sahābi to wake him up.

The Holy Prophet ﷺ did not wake the Sahābi himself, for the fear that he may utter a few incorrect words at him as it normally happens when a person's sleep is disturbed. If this was to happen, then it would have been extremely detrimental for the Sahābi, since this would have been an insult against the Holy Prophet ﷺ. Had the same words been uttered to a Sahābi, it would not have the same effect. Likewise, the Holy Qur'ān can be placed over another Qur'ān, but an ordinary book cannot be placed over a Holy Qur'ān, because this amounts to disrespect. (Ālamgīri)

Eating Together is a Means of Blessings

The Sahābah ﷺ complained to the Holy Prophet ﷺ, "We eat but do not seem to be getting satiated."

The Holy Prophet ﷺ asked them, "Do you all eat individually?" They replied in the affirmative. The Holy Prophet ﷺ then said, "Eat together in a group and read Bismillāh; in it lies blessings." (Abū Dāwūd)

Further, Allāh ﷻ loves that meal from which many people partake of.
(Awāriful-Ma'ārif)

Umar Ibn Abdul Azīz 🌸

Ramadhān was almost over and the streets of Damascus were buzzing with a sense of happiness in preparation for the day of Eid, which was only a few days away. The days were hot, but the markets were crammed with delicacies and people. Men, women and children, mostly from the wealthiest families, filled the market place anxiously searching for the best deals on offer. A few streets away, the son of Umar Ibn Abdul Azīz 🌸, the Caliph of the time, ran into his home crying. The boy's mother instinctively picked him up in her arms and wiped away his tears.

"Why are you crying my dear? Did somebody say something to hurt you?" she asked. But the boy's sobbing only increased. Again she cried, "I told you not to fast because of the heat. Many boys who are older than you are not fasting. Why do you try to fast when you are so young? I am sure that the heat has drained you and you are crying out of thirst?"

Between his sobs, the boy explained, "Mother, I promise you in Allāh's 🌸 Name that I am not thirsty, nor has the fast weakened me."

"Then why are you crying?" she asked and continued, "Eid is only a few days away. You should be looking forward to attending the Eidgāh with your father. You know that Eid is a day of joy."

"But," the boy explained, "This is the reason why I am crying. I know about Eid. All my friends, whose fathers are courtiers and ministers of my father, will be present at the Eidgāh, dressed in new clothing." His mother replied, "You do not need to worry, as I will wash your old clothing with my own hands."

The boy continued, "But mother, all my friends have bought fine new clothes and I am feeling shy about my old clothes. I do not want to go to the Eidgāh." With these words the boy burst into tears. His mother understood her son's request and felt sorry for him. "I will try my best, my dear. Why don't you sleep for a while?" she consoled him.

Shortly thereafter, Umar Ibn Abdul Azīz ﷺ returned home having completed his administrative duties as the Khalīfah. As he was about to lie down for a nap, his wife approached him, "Amīrul Mu'minīn, may my life be sacrificed for you. Eid is approaching and our son is anxious to have a new set of clothing. He arrived home crying about it and I advised him to sleep for a while."

The Caliph lowered his head and said, "You are well aware that I only receive a monthly salary of a hundred Dirhams. With this we purchase our food and pay for the services of a servant. We barely succeed in coming out every month. Rarely do we consider purchasing clothing because the salary is just sufficient for our basic expenses. As far as the public treasury is concerned, the money rightfully belongs to the poor, destitute, orphans and widows. I am only a custodian who has been entrusted to distribute it to the deserving ones. To even think of utilising this wealth is a sin."

"I agree fully, my beloved husband, but the boy does not understand why he has to dress in old clothing while his friends have the best. He has been so deeply saddened by this that you can still notice the stains of tears on his cheeks."

The husband advised, "Fātimah, if you have any personal goods of value, perhaps you should sell them and please him by using the proceeds to purchase a new set of clothing for him."

She answered, "Amīrul Mu'minīn, you have already placed all my jewellery in the public treasury. You even placed the valuable necklace given to me by my father in the public treasury. Besides the love and obedience I have in my heart for you, I have nothing left."

Umar Ibn Abdul Azīz ﷺ again lowered his head and began to ponder deeply. He began to reflect about his past, his childhood, his youth and the luxuries he enjoyed while growing up. He recalled those days when he would not wear an outfit more than once. He recounted the times when the streets where he walked would be perfumed for hours with the scent he applied. He possessed numerous sets of clothing which would lay untouched in his closet. The memories brought tears to his eyes. His wife was saddened at his condition and began to apologise, but he said to her, "Don't worry, Fātimah, I was just recalling the days of my youth."

He then wrote a letter and handed it over to his servant, saying, "Take this to the officer in charge of the public treasury. Take extreme care of whatever he gives you and bring it to me." In the letter he requested that he be given a month's salary in advance. The servant left, but returned a few moments later empty-handed. The servant handed a letter from the treasurer to the Khalīfah. It read, "O Khalīfah of the Muslims, I can fulfil your request with ease, but are you certain that you will live for a month? If not, then why are you taking the rights of the poor, the orphans and the widows on your shoulders?"

The Khalīfah read the letter and with tears in his eyes, remarked, "My honourable treasurer, you have surely saved me from a calamity."

The day of Eid arrived and the streets and homes of Damascus were buzzing with joy. People proceeded to the Eidgāh dressed in their newly purchased outfits. Umar Ibn Abdul Azīz ﷺ also set out holding the hand of his son. Each of them wore an old set of clothing which had been carefully washed. The young boy's face shone brightly, as he walked alongside his father, convinced that the eternal pleasure and comforts of Jannah are far superior to the temporary beauty and adornment of this world.

Our righteous and pious predecessors chose the path of simplicity for themselves and their families, despite the many painful sacrifices they had to endure.

1 Pence Coin

Once, when taking a walk through a park with some friends, we came across a fountain, wherein were numerous 1 pence and 2 pence coins. On noticing this, it came to mind that since the 1 pence coin and the 2 pence coin have negligible value, in fact, no worth or value is really given to these coins. They are generally discarded into a fountain, after some wish is made and if the wish is such, that it would definitely be accomplished with money, then a mere 1 pence or 2 pence would not suffice for the fulfilment of the grand wishes of those who throw with any such hope.

Nevertheless, I presented this analogy to my companions. The value of the 1 pence coin, after having separated itself from the £1 coin, or the £50 note, diminished. It 'depreciated', so to speak. So many pass by such fountains and yet no one considers taking one or a few of those coins. However, if that 1 pence coin attaches itself to a £50 note, then its value and worth is considered just as that £50 note; its value will increase. It is now part of £50.

However, if that 1 pence coin prefers its 'independence' then inevitably, that would be to its own loss. It will then be considered worthless and insignificant and will be discarded in some fountain or thrown on the street.

In a like manner, when the Sālikīn (those who seek Allāh ﷻ) attach themselves to the Ahlullāh (the people of Allāh ﷻ), by keeping their pious company and emulating them in their actions, speech and character, their value increases. When we keep the company of friends of Allāh ﷻ, then Inshā-Allāh, we will, through the blessings of their value, also acquire some worth.

If there is sincerity, the Sālik will also become as valuable and precious. My Shaykh, Maulānā Hakīm Muhammad Akhtar Sāhib ﷺ had given a wonderful analogy when he visited South Africa and observed the sand of the gold mines in Gauteng.

He explained that the sand which remained in the company of gold became 'golden' in colour. Something as ordinary as sand took on the hue and shade of something as precious as gold. So too, one will notice that the sand which contains coal, becomes black in colour.

Hadhrat then compared the golden sand to the person who sincerely befriends and associates with the Ahlullāh. Such a person will not only acquire the same colouring as gold but he will become gold. Those who think they can tread the path to Allāh ﷻ (Sulūk) on their own and also become so valuable, are quite mistaken. Even our honourable and respected Maulānā Jalāluddīn Rūmi ؒ had said, "People addressed me as, 'Molvi' until I attached myself to the blessed company of Shamsuddin Tabrezi ؒ. Then people began addressing me as 'Maulā-e-Rūm' (The Master of Rūm)."

Then again, the Sahābah ؓ became 'Sahābah' because they attached themselves to the blessed and exclusive company of the Holy Prophet ﷺ. This 'Suhbat' (companionship) of the Ahlullāh is the medium of spiritual achievement.

However, great caution should be exercised in choosing a mentor. This warning cannot be emphasised enough. Just the clothes of piety or flowery speech does not make a person a Wali (friend) of Allāh ﷻ. If there is no Dīn in the Shaykh, how will his Murīds change their lives? When the Shaykh is a prisoner of Nafs (ego) and Shaytān, how will it be possible for him to free his Murīds from Nafs and Shaytān?   (Shaykh Yūnus Patel ؒ)

Selflessness and Sympathy

Imām Wāqidi 🌸 was a great scholar of his time. Once he was in great financial difficulty; he was on the verge of poverty. Eid was fast approaching and there was nothing in his home. The elders at home could perhaps bear it patiently, but what about the children?

He says that he was compelled to ask for a loan from a trader friend of his. When his friend saw him, he understood the intention of the visit and placed 1,200 Dirhams in a bag and gave it to Imām Wāqidi 🌸.

When he reached home, a Hāshimi friend of his came by, who was also in a state of poverty and need. Imām Wāqidi 🌸 said to his wife, "Distribute the contents of the bag into two equal parts and in this way, both our needs will be sufficed."

His wife said, "This is strange! You have been to a normal layman who gave you 1,200 Dirhams and you are only giving him half of what a layman has given you! Do give him the entire bag."

Without any hesitation, Imām Wāqidi 🌸 gave the entire sealed bag to his Hāshimi friend, without even opening it. The Hāshimi took the bag.

Meanwhile, the trader friend of Imām Wāqidi 🌸 stopped by this Hāshimi, and said, "Eid is very close by and there is nothing in the home. I would like a loan." The Hāshimi offered him the very same sealed bag.

When the trader saw his own bag, which was still sealed, he was astonished and sought to investigate the circumstances surrounding it.

He left the bag with the Hāshimi and came to Imām Wāqidi ﷺ, who narrated the entire episode to him. In reality, the trader also had nothing besides the bag and its contents and he gave the entire bag to Imām Wāqidi ﷺ. Then, he sought a loan for himself, which is why he went to the Hāshimi. When the Hāshimi offered him the bag, the entire secret was revealed.

When this wonderful incident of selflessness and sympathy reached the Wazīr (leader) of the country, Yahyā Ibn Khālid, he took 10,000 Dīnārs and said, "Two thousand is for Imām Wāqidi ﷺ, two thousand is for the Hāshimi, two thousand is for the trader and the remaining four thousand is for Imām Wāqidi's ﷺ wife, who is the most worthy and deserving of it."

"And they prefer others over themselves, even though poverty be their lot." (59:9)

These were those people who appreciated the value of Islamic character, such that when a non-Muslim saw their behaviour, he accepted Islām willingly.

Have you considered why the Wazīr, Yahyā Ibn Khālid gave the wife of Imām Wāqidi ﷺ the most of all (4,000 Dirhams)?

A Trustworthy Man

A businessman who lived centuries ago related the following story:

My business was doing so well one year and I had earned so much money that I decided to take a break from business and dedicate some time to worship. I joined a group that was heading off to make the annual pilgrimage to Makkah Mukarramah. I took along two bags which I tied around my waist. In them, I kept money and some precious jewels in case need should arise during the journey.

When I stopped to relieve myself at some point during the journey, my belt loosened from the waist and the bags fell to the ground. However, I only realised that the bags were missing many miles later; we had travelled far enough that I had every reason to lose hope of finding the bags again. Nevertheless, losing the money and the jewels had no effect on me whatsoever; after all, I was still rich and I knew that since I was travelling to worship Allāh ﷻ, He would soon recompense me for what I had lost.

After the pilgrimage was over and I was back in my homeland, my situation in life worsened. Every business venture I embarked upon ended up in failure, until I finally lost everything. Feeling the disgrace of failure and poverty, I fled with my family from my homeland and we wandered for many years in a state of poverty.

The hardship of poverty became even more difficult to bear when one night, my wife gave birth to a baby boy. My wife had lost much blood and needed medical attention as well as food. All that I had with me, however, was two small coins. It was a rainy night and so despite my wife's weakness, I took her to an abandoned inn, where I asked her to rest while I went out in search of food and help.

I wandered aimlessly for a while until I came across a store; I didn't go inside, however, for what could I hope to buy with only two small coins. Seeing my miserable state, the storekeeper came out and began talking to me. When I told him my situation, he felt sorry for me and in exchange for the two coins I had, he gave me milk and oil, both of the best kinds. He also lent me a container in which I placed the supplies.

I then headed back towards my wife, feeling content in that I could at least give her some nourishment. Nothing was going right though; I slipped on the way. The container shattered as it fell to the ground and all that was in it spilled onto the ground. There I sat, a miserable and wretched creature. Although I had endured poverty for many years, I was never so hopeless and downtrodden as I was at that point in time. I began to cry; apparently, I was crying out loud, for a man opened the window of his home, near to where I was seated, and said, "Woe unto you! Why are you crying? And why do you not let us go to sleep?"

I explained to him my story, or just that part of it that took place in the last two days or so. He looked at me in surprise and said, "All of this crying for two small coins?" I became even more miserable after hearing what he said. I answered, "By Allāh ﷻ, I am not crying over the money I lost; I am crying out of mercy for my wife and my own self. At this very minute, my wife is dying of hunger. By Allāh ﷻ, I performed pilgrimage in such and such year and I owned such and such amount of wealth. I lost a great deal of that wealth when I lost two bags containing money and precious jewels. I didn't care about that loss then. Do you think now that I will cry over two small coins? Indeed, I ask Allāh ﷻ to protect me from such humiliation. And do not insult me, or else you might become afflicted as I am afflicted now."

The man, getting excited for some reason, said to me, "Describe your bags to me." I approached him and with tears falling from my eyes, I said, "Here I am standing in the rain and to add insult to injury, you want to ask me about my bags? How will that benefit me?" He insisted that I describe them to him and when I indicated to him that I was about to leave, he held on to me so I had no choice but to fulfil his request. After I described the bags and their contents to him, he asked me to enter and said, "Where is your wife?" I told him that she was resting in an abandoned inn; he then sent his servant to go and fetch her.

When my wife arrived, she was taken to the female members of the household, who took care of her, providing for her every need. Their generosity was not limited to my wife, for I was given a new set of clean garments to wear; I was told to take a shower and then to wear them. When I was clean and was finished freshening up, the man said, "Stay with me for a few days." He was so hospitable and kind that I ended up staying for ten days. Each day he gave me 10 Dīnārs, explaining that they were gifts. I must admit that I was somewhat taken aback; he first seemed cold to me when I was standing out in the rain and now he was so kind and generous.

On the 10th day, he began to talk more openly with me, perhaps noticing that I finally felt at home under his hospitable care. He asked me what I did for a living and I told them that I had once been a businessman. He said that he had some money to invest and he wanted to know whether I would be willing to do business on his behalf and thus become his partner. I immediately agreed. He took out 100 Dinārs, gave them to me and finalised the agreement. Not only had he been a hospitable host, but he now also gave me a new source of income. I thanked Allāh ﷻ for having made me rich again.

The man then asked me to sit down, after which he proceeded to take out two bags I was very surprised to see that they were the very same bags, that I had lost many years ago. He said, "Do you recognise these?" When I saw the bags, I immediately fainted. One hour passed before I finally regained consciousness. He then said to me, "I have been keeping this safe for so many years. On the night that I met you, when you gave an account of your story, I asked you to describe the bags to me. Upon hearing your description, I immediately knew that I had finally found the owner of the bags. However, seeing your miserable state, I did not want to tell you about your bags right away, fearing that the shock would be too much for you. So, I asked you to stay with me and each day I gave you 10 Dinārs not from my own wealth, but from your wealth - from your own bags. Take your bags and all of your money and jewels and forgive me for having deceived you, though I only did so for your welfare." I thanked him and prayed for him. I then took the bags, returned to my homeland and using his money as well as mine, I began to do business again. Only a few years passed by before my newly found friend/business partner and I became very rich and prosperous.

All praise is for Allāh ﷻ, Lord of all that exists.

Miracle of Sayyidunā Abū Bakr As-Siddīq 🕊

Abdur Rahmān Ibn Abū Bakr As Siddīq 🕊 narrates that the people of Suffa were very poor. These were the Companions 🕊 that were unmarried and had no home to go to, so they sought shelter in the Masjid near to one of the houses of the Holy Prophet 🕊.

One day, the Holy Prophet 🕊 said, "Whoever has food for two, then let him take a third (person) with him (to share his food) and whoever has food for four, then let him take a fifth (or) sixth (person) with him." Here, the Holy Prophet 🕊 was instructing some of the wealthier Companions 🕊 to share their meals with the people of Suffa. However, the Holy Prophet 🕊, as was always the case, made matters easy for everyone. He did not instruct one person to take on the responsibility of taking all the people of Suffa at once but rather, he distributed the responsibility of feeding the people of Suffa between all of the wealthier Sahābahs 🕊.

One night, Sayyidunā Abū Bakr 🕊 took three people with him while the Holy Prophet 🕊 took ten people with him to share his food. Though Sayyidunā Abū Bakr 🕊 had guests of his own, he had dinner with the Holy Prophet 🕊 for he was ever eager to be in his company besides, his son, Abdur Rahmān 🕊 was home to serve the guests. Sayyidunā Abū Bakr 🕊 stayed until he had prayed Ishā Salāh and then later returned to his home.

When he entered his home, his wife asked, "What has kept you away from your guests?" Sayyidunā Abū Bakr 🕊 said, "Did you not feed them dinner?" She replied, "They refused to eat until you came. The food was served to them, but they refused to eat it." They did this out of modesty and out of respect for Sayyidunā Abū Bakr ⏾. Meanwhile, Abdur Rahmān ⏾ hid himself fearing that his father will be angry with him. Indeed, Sayyidunā Abū Bakr ⏾ was upset and when he found Abdur Rahmān ⏾, he severely reproached him. He also reproached the guests for not having eaten earlier and he even said, "By Allāh, I will never eat this (i.e. you will eat all this and I will not touch a morsel)."

Abdur Rahmān ⏾ later recounted, "By Allāh, we would not take a morsel (from that meal) except that more of it appeared from the bottom of the dish, until finally everyone was satisfied. And there was more food there than there had been in the first place." This was a miracle that occurred by the permission of Allāh ﷻ for Sayyidunā Abū Bakr ⏾.

Amazed by what he saw, Sayyidunā Abū Bakr ⏾ asked his wife, "O Sister of Banū Farās, what is this?" She confirmed for him what he saw. "No, this is the delight of my eyes. It is indeed three times more now than it was to begin with!"

In Islām, if one makes an oath not to do something but then realises that it is best to do that thing, then one may do it, except that he has to make atonement for breaking his oath. Thus, seeing that the food was blessed, Sayyidunā Abū Bakr ⏾ ate from it and said, "That (i.e. my making an oath not to eat this food) was indeed from Shaytān." Sayyidunā Abū Bakr ⏾ took a bite and then took the rest to the Holy Prophet ﷺ. Now that the dish was with the Holy Prophet ﷺ, twelve people agreed to partake of its contents and return with a number of guests to share it with them. They did so and everyone eventually ate from a dish that had initially contained only enough food for three or four people!

Sayyidunā Sa'd Ibn Abī Waqqās ⬥

A number of years after the Holy Prophet ⬥ had passed away, the people of Kūfa complained to the Leader of the Believers, Sayyidunā Umar ⬥ about their governor, Sayyidunā Sa'd Ibn Abī Waqqās ⬥. Sayyidunā Umar ⬥ replaced Sayyidunā Sa'd ⬥ with a new governor, Sayyidunā Ammār Ibn Yāsir ⬥, in the hope that the population of Kūfa would somehow become manageable under the leadership of a new governor. Such was the way of Sayyidunā Umar ⬥ that he did not hesitate to re-place his governors. That is not to say that he disliked or distrusted all of the governors that he removed; to the contrary, he was simply looking for what worked and so sometimes, however worthy a governor was, he might not have been suitable to a particular group of citizens.

The people of Kūfa were unsatisfied with Sayyidunā Sa'd ⬥, for they sent news to Sayyidunā Umar ⬥ that when Sa'd ⬥ led them in prayer, he per-formed the prayer in an incorrect manner. Sayyidunā Umar ⬥ sent for him and when the two of them were face to face, Sayyidunā Umar ⬥ said, "O' Abū Ishāq, they claim that you pray incorrectly."

"Verily," began Sayyidunā Sa'd ⬥, "I led them in prayer in exactly the same manner that the Messenger of Allāh ⬥ prayed; indeed, I did not decrease anything from his prayer. (For example) when I lead them in Ishā prayer, I prolong the first two units and shorten the last two units."

"That is what one would think about you, O' Abū Ishāq," said Sayyidunā Umar ⬥. Thereafter, Sayyidunā Umar ⬥ reassuringly sent Sayyidunā Sa'd ⬥ back, but he also sent with Sayyidunā Sa'd ⬥ a number of men to conduct a survey in Kūfa, the purpose of which was to see how satisfied the people of Kūfa were with their governor. These emissaries went to every single Masjid in Kūfa to ask about Sayyidunā Sa'd's 🙵 performance as a governor and everyone responded with praise for Sayyidunā Sa'd 🙵. However, when Sayyidunā Umar's 🙵 emissaries went to the Masjid of Banū Abs clan, a man named Usāmah Ibn Qatādah stood up and said, "Since you are asking us to speak, I would like to say that Sa'd 🙵 would not join the military units (that would go for special missions); also, he would distribute (public wealth) unfairly; furthermore, he was not fair when he pronounced his judgements!"

When Sayyidunā Sa'd 🙵 heard about what the man accused him of, he said, "By Allāh, I will invoke against him three things (to befall on him); O' Allāh, if that slave of yours was lying and if he stood up only to be seen and heard (in order to gain a reputation), prolong his life, prolong his poverty and cause him to be faced with trials."

Later on in life when Usāmah Ibn Qatādah became old and frail, he was asked about his pitiable condition. He replied, "I am a very old man being put to trial; I have been afflicted by the supplication of Sa'd Ibn Abī Waqqās 🙵." Abdul-Malik said that he saw Usāmah Ibn Qatādah in his final years. He saw Usāmah's eyebrows dropping down over his eyes; that is how old he was. He also saw Usāmah stalking young girls in the roads in order to wink at them and touch them.

Words of Wisdom of Sayyidunā Ali ﷺ

1. The punishment of involving yourself in the love of material things is the deprivation of true love for Allāh ﷻ.

2. Miserliness is the clothing of dishonour.

3. Do not be satisfied with the results of that person whose heart is not in his work.

4. It is easier to turn a mountain into dust than to create love in the heart that is filled with hatred.

5. The person who follows his desires will surely get lost.

6. Bravery is that you exercise patience for a little while.

7. Moderation is the best status in all affairs.

8. Your best friend is that person who assists you the most in the time of your needs.

9. It is better to refrain from sins than to seek forgiveness later.

10. The person who is ensnared by jealousy will be ensnared by a bad ending.

11. Many diseases and problems are due to extravagance.

12. An intelligent enemy is sometimes better than a foolish friend.

13. Ability to do something is good fortune and helplessness is misfortune.

14. The person who points out and looks for faults in others, opens the door of exposing his faults to others.

15. For the person who assists a brother at times of difficulty, Allāh ﷻ will assist him in his time of need.

16. The person who is saved from the tongue of others is fortunate.

17. The person who saves himself from vulgar language will find success.

18. Every act that is beneficial is Sadaqah (charity).

19. Many strange people are better than your own relatives.

20. Many of the drowned are those who have been sunk in the sea of ignorance.

21. Many are the Ulamā (learned) whom the world has destroyed.

22. The best of your wealth is that which is of most benefit to you in times of need.

23. Whoever loves this world, he is in reality accumulating his wealth for others.

24. During the day man's actions are always changing, so appreciate those days in which you are able to do good actions.

25. At the time of reaching the extreme of difficulty and hardship, then know that the time of ease has to come.

26. The man who is living in ease cannot appreciate the level of difficulties of others.

27. The person who has very little wealth and means of happiness will only have ease and comfort at death.

28. Sometimes, a little increases and becomes a lot and sometimes a great deal decreases to nothing.

29. To ask brings dishonour and to give creates love.

30. A little, well earned which satisfies your needs will suffice you better than a lot which is spent extravagantly.

31. The greater the degree of happiness, the more, at the end of it will be your difficulty, loss or grief.

32. The company of bad or evil people cause a good person to also be regarded as evil.

33. Some are great people but people do not value them.

34. A respected person always remains honourable even if he is afflicted with difficulties.

35. He will not be lost who keeps on asking the way.

36. A person will not be perplexed who makes Mashwara (consultation) with others.

37. A cautious and intelligent person is he who does not rely on his own opinion and judgement.

38. A person who is satisfied with his own actions will have many that dislike him.

39. For the person whose self is precious in his own eyes, his desires will be valueless to him.

40. For the person who regards minor difficulties as major, Allāh ﷻ will afflict him with major difficulties and problems

Remember Your Role Model

When becoming humiliated, remember the
Holy Prophet ﷺ in Tā'if.

When being starved, remember the Holy Prophet ﷺ tying two stones to
his stomach in the Battle of Khandaq (Trench).

When becoming angry, remember the Holy Prophet's ﷺ control of anger
on the martyrdom of his beloved Uncle Sayyidunā Hamza ؓ.
When losing a tooth, remember the Holy Prophet's ﷺ tooth in the battle
of Uhud.

When bleeding from any part of the body, remember the Holy Prophet's
ﷺ body covered in blood on his return from Tā'if.

When feeling lonely, remember the Holy Prophet's ﷺ seclusion in
Mount Hira.

When feeling tired in Salāh, remember the Holy Prophet's ﷺ blessed feet
in Tahajjud.

When being prickled with thorns, remember the
Holy Prophet's ﷺ pain from Abū Lahab's wife.

When being troubled by neighbours, remember the old woman who
would empty rubbish on the Holy Prophet ﷺ.

When losing a child, remember the
Holy Prophet's ﷺ son, Ibrāhīm.

When beginning a long journey, remember the Holy Prophet's ﷺ long
journey to Madīnah Munawwarah.

When going against a Sunnah, remember the Holy Prophet's ﷺ interces-
sion,(Ummati, Ummati, Ummati-My Ummah, My Ummah,
My Ummah).

Before shaving your beard, remember the Holy Prophet's ﷺ face reject-
ing the two beardless Iranians.

When falling into an argument with your wife, remember the Holy
Prophet's ﷺ encounter with Sayyidah Āʾishah ﷺ
and Sayyidah Hafsah ﷺ

When experiencing less food in the house, remember the Holy Prophet's
ﷺ days of poverty.

When experiencing poverty, remember the Holy Prophet's ﷺ advice to
Ashāb-e-Suffa (People of Suffa).

When losing a family member, remember the Holy Prophet's ﷺ departure from this world.

When becoming an orphan, remember the Holy Prophet's ﷺ age at six.

When sponsoring an orphan, remember the Holy Prophet's ﷺ sponsor
for Sayyidunā Zayd Ibn Hāritha ﷺ.

When fearing an enemy, remember the Holy Prophet's ﷺ saying to Sayyidunā Abū Bakr ؓ on Mount Thawr.

Whatever situation you may find yourself in, remember your role model, the best of creation, **Prophet Muhammad ﷺ.**

Sayyidunā Ali's ؓ Intelligence

Two men left a substantial amount of money in the custody of a Quraishi lady. When leaving their Amānah (trust money), they instructed her to return it to them only when they both asked for it together. Under no circumstances should she hand over the Amānah to only one of them.

After a year, one of them appeared claiming that his partner had died. He demanded the return of the money. The lady refused and reminded him of the condition the two had fixed for the return of the Amānah. The man was stubborn in his demand. He refused to leave. He caused a big disturbance in the neighbourhood, complaining loudly. The residents forced the lady to return the money. Ultimately, she relented.

After some time, the second man appeared and requested the Amānah. The lady was confused. She explained what had transpired, but he refused to accept her explanation, saying that she was guilty of violating the agreement. He demanded that she compensates him since she was at fault.

The dispute was brought to Sayyidunā Ali ؓ. After he heard both parties, he concluded that the two had tricked the lady. He said to the man:

"Did the two of you not stipulate that she should hand over the

Amānah only when both come?"

The man readily agreed. Sayyidunā Ali ﷺ said:
"Your money is by me. Bring your friend and collect it."

The device of the fraud was thus unsuccessful.

Abdullāh Ibn Mubārak's ﷺ Victory

It has been narrated that Abdullāh Ibn Mubārak ﷺ divided his life into three parts; one year for pilgrimage, one year for Jihād and one year for teaching.

Once while out in battle, he could not penetrate the fort of his enemies. That night, he slept with the worry of how to penetrate the fort of his enemies. Rasūlullāh ﷺ appeared in his dream saying, "O' Abdullāh! What is worrying you?" He replied, "We cannot overpower the enemies." Rasūlullāh ﷺ said, "Use the Miswāk when performing Wudhu."

When he awakened from his sleep, he made Wudhu using the Miswāk. He commanded the soldiers to do the same. They carried out this command. The guardians of the fort saw them using the Miswāk. Allāh ﷺ placed such fear in their hearts that they came down and told their commanders that the army that had come were cannibals and that they were sharpening their teeth so that if they overpowered them, they would eat them. Allāh ﷺ placed this fear in their hearts also.

They sent a messenger to the Muslims asking, "Do you want goods, money or lives?"

Abdullāh Ibn Mubārak ﷺ replied, "We don't want wealth or lives. We want you all to accept Islam so that you may be saved." By the blessing of practicing the Sunnah of the Miswāk, they all accepted Islām.

Malcolm X Goes For Hajj

When he was in Makkah, Al-Hājj Mālik Shabāz (Malcolm X) wrote a letter to his loyal assistants in Harlem from his heart:

"Never have I witnessed such sincere hospitality and overwhelming spirit of true brotherhood as is practised by people of all colours and races here in this ancient Holy Land, the home of Ibrāhīm السلام عليه , Muhammad ﷺ and all other Prophets of the Holy Scriptures. For the past week, I have been utterly speechless and spellbound by the graciousness I have seen displayed all around me by people of all colours.

I have been blessed to visit the Holy City of Makkah, I have made my seven circuits around the Ka'bah. I have drank from the well of Zam Zam. I ran seven times back and forth between the hills of Mount Safā and Marwah. I have prayed in the ancient city of Minā and I have prayed in Arafāt.

There were tens of thousands of pilgrims from all over the world. They were of all colours, from blue-eyed blondes to black skinned Africans. But we were all participating in the same ritual, displaying a spirit of unity and brotherhood that my experiences in America had led me to believe never could exist between white and non white.

America needs to understand Islām, because this is the one religion

69

that erases from its society the race problem. Throughout my travels in the Muslim world, I have met, talked to, and even eaten, with people who in America, would have been considered white - but the white attitude was removed from their minds by the religion of Islām. I have never before seen sincere and true brotherhood practised by all colours together, irrespective of their colour.

You may be shocked by these words coming from me. But on this pilgrimage, what I have seen and experienced, has forced me to rearrange much of my thought-patterns previously held and to toss aside some of my previous conclusions. This was not too difficult for me. Despite my firm convictions, I have always been a man who tries to face facts and to accept the reality of life as new experience and new knowledge unfolds it. I have always kept an open mind, which is necessary to the flexibility that must go hand in hand with every form of intelligent search for truth.

During the past eleven days here in the Muslim world, I have eaten from the same plate, drunk from the same glass and slept on the same rug, while praying to the same God, with fellow Muslims, whose eyes were the bluest of blue, whose hair were the blondest of blond and whose skin were the whitest of white. And in the words and in the actions and in the deeds of the white Muslims, I felt the same sincerity that I felt among the black African Muslims of Nigeria, Sudan and Ghana.

We were truly all the same (brothers), because their belief in One God had removed the white from their minds, the white from their behaviour, and the white from their attitude. I could see from this, that perhaps if white Americans could accept the Oneness of God, then perhaps too, they could accept in reality the oneness of man and cease to measure and hinder and harm others in terms of their 'differences' in colour.

With racism plaguing America like an incurable cancer, the so-called 'Christian' white American heart should be more receptive to a proven solution to such a destructive problem. Perhaps it could be in time to save America from imminent disaster, the same destruction brought upon Germany by racism that eventually destroyed the Germans themselves.

Each hour in the Holy Land enables me to have greater spiritual insights into what is happening in America between black and white. The American Negro never can be blamed for his racial animosities (hostilities); he is only reacting to four hundred years of the conscious racism of the American whites. But as racism leads America up the suicide path, I do believe, from the experiences that I have had with them, that the whites of the younger generation, in the colleges and universities, will see the handwriting on the walls and many of them will turn to the spiritual path of truth. The only way left for America to ward off the disaster that racism inevitably must lead to.

Never have I been so highly honoured. Never have I been made to feel more humble and unworthy. Who would believe the blessings that have been heaped upon an American Negro? A few nights ago, a man who would be called in America a white man, a United Nations diplomat, an ambassador, a companion of kings, gave me his hotel suite, his bed. Never would I have even thought of dreaming that I would ever be a recipient of such honours, honours that in America would be bestowed upon a king, not a Negro."

All praise is due to Allāh ﷻ, the Lord of all the worlds.
Al-Hājj Mālik Shabāz (Malcolm X)

(From the Autobiography of Malcolm X)

The Forgotten History of Madrasah Sawlatiyya in Makkah Mukarramah

Shaykh Rahmatullāh Kayrānvi ﷺ (1818-1891) was a scholar of the Indian origin. He is best known for his masterpiece 'Izhār-ul Haq' - 'The Truth Revealed. He was a honourable warrior in the battle for freedom which took place in 1857. The uprising failed due to various reasons.

Shaykh Kayrānvi ﷺ (who also happened to be a descendant of the third caliph, Sayyidunā Uthmān Ibn Affān ﷺ) migrated to Makkah via Mocha, Yemen. He arrived aboard a ship from Bombay, India. He then walked the distance of about 600 miles from Mocha, Yemen to Makkah which took him about 2 years.

After having migrated to the sacred land, he intended to set up an Islamic seminary but scarcity of resources proved to be a real hurdle. Then the help of Allāh ﷻ descended.

Begum Sawlatun Nisā, a woman known for her generosity was a descendant of the pious Muslim ruler of the kingdom of Mysore in South India, Tipu Sultān ﷺ (1750-1799). Begum Sawlatun Nisā happened to visit the Holy land (probably for the pilgrimage) around that time.

While there, she received news regarding the setting up of the institute. She supported the proposal and donated a considerable amount of 30,000 (currency is not known, although 30,000 rupees at that time too would have been a lot of money) for the noble cause. It was then that Shaykh Rahmatullāh Kayrānvi ﷺ attributed the school to her and named it **'Madrasah Sawlatiyya'** (founded in 1875 / 1292 H) which continues to exist even to this day (a span of 138 years). Tens of thousands have been educated in the Islamic sciences since then.

$$مَنْ دَلَّ عَلَى خَيْرٍ فَلَه مِثْلُ أَجْرِ فَاعِلِه (رَوَاهُ مُسْلِمٌ)$$

"He who guides to what is good will have a reward equivalent to that of him who acts upon it." (Muslim)

Shaykh Kayrānvi ﷺ passed away 16 years later in 1891. Not much is known about Begum Sawlatun Nisā after this, not even her death. She will probably be nothing more than a mere footnote in the pages of history. Yet, in the light of the Holy Qur'ān and the above Hadīth, I leave it to you to calculate the rewards they have and continue to acquire in the Hereafter.

Companions Grief at the Demise of the Holy Prophet ﷺ

Sayyidah Umme Salamah ﷺ says, "When we (the wives of the Holy Prophet ﷺ) gathered together and were weeping over the demise of the Holy Prophet ﷺ, we did not have a wink of sleep. The blessed body of the Holy Prophet ﷺ was still in our rooms and we consoled each other every time we saw him lying on the bed.

When we suddenly heard the sound of shovels digging the Holy Prophet's ﷺ grave just before dawn, we started crying out of grief and the people in the Masjid also started crying. This caused all of Madīnah Munawwarah to shudder.

When Sayyidunā Bilāl ⁎ called out the Fajr Adhān and took the name of the Holy Prophet ⁎, he burst out crying. This added to our grief and the people started going towards the grave. O what a calamity it was! Every calamity that befell us afterwards paled into insignificance when we thought about the calamity of the Holy Prophet's ⁎ demise."

One can hardly imagine the sorrow and grief the Companions ⁎ went through on the departure of our Holy Prophet ⁎.

Sayyidunā Abū Dhu'aib Hudhali ⁎ says, "When I arrived in Madīnah Munawwarah, the wailing of the people of Madīnah pulsated like the calls of 'Labbayk' from the people performing Hajj. 'What is the matter?' I enquired. They informed me that the Holy Prophet ⁎ had passed away." (Hayātus Sahābah)

Sayyidunā Ubaidullāh Ibn Umair ⁎ reports that when the Holy Prophet ⁎ passed away, the governor of Makkah was Sayyidunā Attāb Ibn Usayd ⁎. When the news of Rasūlullāh's ⁎ demise reached the inhabitants of Makkah, the people in the Masjid burst out crying. Sayyidunā Attāb ⁎ left Makkah and went to one of its valleys. Sayyidunā Suhail Ibn Amr ⁎ approached him and told him to address the people. He said, "I cannot speak after the demise of the Holy Prophet ⁎."

Sayyidunā Abū Ja'far ⁎ says, "After the demise of the Holy Prophet ⁎, I never saw (Sayyidah) Fātimah ⁎ laugh."

Sayyidunā Abū Bakr ☙ said after the demise of the Holy Prophet ☙, "Today we have lost revelation and speech from Allāh ☙."

I would like to share with our readers the couplets recited by Sayyidah Safiyyah ☙ (the aunt of the Holy Prophet ☙) in memory of the Holy Prophet ☙. These couplets will clearly demonstrate to us the love the Companions ☙ had for the Holy Prophet ☙.

Urwa ☙ reports that Sayyidah Safiyyah ☙ recited a few couplets in memory of the Holy Prophet ☙. The meaning of the couplets are,

"My heart grieves and I have spent the night like he who has lost everything.

I have stayed awake all night like the one whose every possession has been looted.

It is all because of my grief and remorse that I cannot sleep.

If only I was also given the cup of death to sip from.

When we came to the family of Muhammad ☙, the hair on the back of our necks turned white (with grief).

When we saw his rooms had become deserted, after him there was none there to live life as a stranger, because of this, a deep grief has come to me, mixing in my heart, filling it with fear."

Sayyidah Safiyyah ☙ also recited the following couplets,

"Do listen, Rasūlullāh ﷺ! You had been the one to give us ease. You had been good to us and never harsh.

Our Prophet ﷺ had always been good and forgiving towards us.

Today everyone who wishes to weep should respond.

By my life! It is not because of his death that I weep for my Prophet ﷺ.

It is rather because of the hardships that are to come after him.

Because of the loss of Muhammad ﷺ and because of the love for him, my heart has been branded by a hot iron.

O' Fātimah! May the Rabb of Muhammad ﷺ shower His special mercies on the body that had taken up residence in Yathrib.

I am looking at Hasan whom you have left as an orphan. Making him cry and call out for his grandfather who has gone so far.

I am ready to sacrifice for Rasūlullāh ﷺ, my mother, my aunt, my uncle, myself and all of my near and dear relatives.

You had endured much and conveyed the Message with truth.

You had left the world with the Dīn firm, apparent and clear.

Had the Rabb (Lord) of the throne kept you alive with us, we would have been most fortunate but His decision is final.

May peace and greetings from Allāh ﷻ be showered on you, as you are entered happily into the everlasting gardens."

May Allāh ﷻ inculcate the love of the Holy Prophet ﷺ in our hearts. Āmīn!

Sayyidah Fātimah ؓ said to Sayyidunā Anas Ibn Mālik ؓ, "O Anas! How did your heart allow you to throw earth on the body of the Holy Prophet ﷺ when he was buried?"

The whole thing was difficult for them; the washing of the Holy Prophet ﷺ, the burial of the Holy Prophet ﷺ and the death of the Holy Prophet ﷺ. That is why the Holy Prophet ﷺ said, "If one of you is afflicted with a calamity, then let him remember his calamity by me (i.e. by my death), for indeed, it is the greatest of calamities."

The greatest calamity that can befall a Muslim has already happened and that is the death of the Holy Prophet ﷺ. Whatever happens to you after that is going to be small compared to the loss of the Holy Prophet ﷺ.

Sayyidunā Anas Ibn Mālik ؓ says, "I witnessed two days in my life; one of the best days in my life and one of the worst days in my life. The best day was when the Holy Prophet ﷺ came to Madīnah Munawwarah and that was a day everything was bright. The worst day was the day the Holy Prophet ﷺ passed away and that was a dark day."

Sayyidunā Anas ؓ also says, "By the time we were dusting our hands after the burial of the Holy Prophet ﷺ, we already felt that our hearts were different." The hearts were different because of the death of the Holy Prophet ﷺ.

One day Sayyidunā Abū Bakr ؓ and Sayyidunā Umar ؓ decided to visit Sayyidah Umme Ayman ؅. She started to cry. They asked her, "Why are you crying?" She said, "I am crying because there is no revelation."

It was not only the Holy Prophet ﷺ that they were missing but also the revelation from the skies. Imagine living in a time when the Holy Qur'ān was being revealed with verses that you are hearing for the first time in your life.

The Holy Prophet ﷺ did not leave behind any inheritance. The Holy Prophet ﷺ lived for his Ummah, serving Allāh ﷻ. The Holy Prophet ﷺ passed away from this Dunyā clean. He only left behind a white mule, his weapons and land that he left for the travellers as Sadaqah.

Muhammad Ibn Ishāq ؓ says, "The Holy Prophet ﷺ passed away on the 12th of Rabīul Awwal; The same day in which he made Hijrah to Madīnah Munawwarah 10 years previously. The Holy Prophet ﷺ lived exactly 10 years in Madīnah Munawwarah. The Holy Prophet ﷺ died aged 63, Sayyidunā Abū Bakr ؓ died at 63 and Sayyidunā Umar ؓ died at 63. They followed the footsteps of Rasūlullāh ﷺ even in his death."

We ask Allāh ﷻ to make us from those who truly love the Holy Prophet ﷺ, to make us of those who follow his Sunnah, to make us of those who would be raised up with him on the Day of Judgement and to make us of those who will drink from his hands at Al Kawthar. We ask Allāh ﷻ to admit us with him in Paradise. Āmīn!

Dear Readers, review the Sīrah, read it again, follow it, love Muhammad ﷺ. Be concerned about the Ummah, just like the Holy Prophet ﷺ was.

Remember the Holy Prophet ﷺ lived and died for you. Remember the Holy Prophet ﷺ left a lot of the enjoyment of the Dunyā (world) for the sake of having Islām come to you. Who among all humanity do we owe more to than the Holy Prophet ﷺ? We owe a lot to the Holy Prophet ﷺ. Everything we know about Islām came to us through him, so how much do we owe him? The least we can do in recognition for what the Holy Prophet ﷺ did for us, is that we sent Durood on the Holy Prophet ﷺ:

اللّٰهُمَّ صَلِّ عَلٰى مُحَمَّدٍ كُلَّمَا ذَكَرَهُ الذَّا كِرُوْن وَصَلِّ عَلٰى مُحَمَّدٍ كُلَّمَا غَفَلَ عَنْ ذِكْرِهِ الْغَافِلُوْن

Sayyidunā Mu'āwiya ﷺ

Sayyidunā Mu'āwiya ﷺ was born five years before the proclamation of Prophethood, meaning the Holy Prophet ﷺ was thirty five years old at the time. From childhood, already the signs of determination and nobility were visible in him. Consequently, once while still young, his father Abū Sufyān ﷺ looked at him and said, "My son has a grand head and is worthy of being the head of his people." His mother, Hinda ﷺ heard this remark and commented, "What! Only the head of his people? I will weep if he does not lead the entire Arab Nation."

He would write the Holy Prophet's ﷺ letters and his statements. Due to his writing down of Wahī, he was known as 'Kātib-ul Wahī' (Scribe of Divine Revelation). Concerning the writers of Wahī, Allāh ﷺ says,

فِيْ صُحُفٍ مُّكَرَّمَةٍ مَّرْفُوْعَةٍ مُّطَهَّرَةٍ بِأَيْدِيْ سَفَرَةٍ كِرَامٍ بَرَرَةٍ

"Written on honoured pages, exalted, purified, by the hands of Scribes, honoured righteous." (80:13-15)

The historian Ibn Hazm ⚜ writes, "From amongst the scribes of the Holy Prophet ⚜, Sayyidunā Zaid Ibn Thābit ⚜ was most frequently with Allāh's Messenger ⚜. Second only to him was Sayyidunā Mu'āwiya ⚜. These two were with the Holy Prophet ⚜ day and night and did no other work."

In the famous book 'Jāmi Tirmizi', it is reported that the Holy Prophet ⚜ made the following Du'ā for him, "O' Allāh ⚜, make Mu'āwiya a guide (for others), one who is himself rightly guided and a means of guidance for people."

In another Hadīth, the Holy Prophet ⚜ made the following supplication for him, saying, "O' Allāh ⚜, teach Mu'āwiya accounting and protect him from the punishment of Jahannam." The renowned Sahābi, Sayyidunā Amr Ibnul-Ās ⚜ says that he heard the Holy Prophet ⚜ say, "O' Allāh ⚜, teach him the Qur'ān, grant him a strong hold upon the lands and save him from the torment of Jahannam."

In addition to this, Sayyidunā Mu'āwiya ⚜ himself said, "Once, I went to fetch some water for the Holy Prophet ⚜ to perform Wudhu. Upon completion of his Wudhu with this water, the Holy Prophet ⚜ looked at me and said, 'O' Mu'āwiya, when governorship is given to you (i.e. you become a ruler), then remain fearful of Allāh ⚜ and be just.' In some narrations, the Holy Prophet ⚜ is reported to have added, "Whosoever does good deeds, pay attention to him and be good. Whosoever does any evil, then overlook it." After narrating this Hadīth, Sayyidunā Mu'āwiya ⚜ says, "After this statement of the Holy Prophet ⚜, the thought stuck to my mind that I would definitely be tried with this responsibility. Consequently, events transpired likewise (i.e. I was made the ruler)."

One narration even has it, that once the Holy Prophet ﷺ consulted with Sayyidunā Abū Bakr and Sayyidunā Umar regarding some affair but when both were unable to propose a suitable solution, the Holy Prophet ﷺ said, "Call Mu'āwiya and present the case before him because he is very authoritative (in counselling) and trustworthy (i.e. he would not give wrong advice)."

There is yet another Hadīth wherein the Holy Prophet ﷺ mounted his conveyance, seating Sayyidunā Mu'āwiya behind him. After a short while, the Holy Prophet ﷺ asked him, "O', Mu'āwiya which part of your body is touching mine?" He replied, "O' Rasūl of Allāh ﷺ, my abdomen (and chest) is touching your blessed body." Upon hearing this, the Holy Prophet ﷺ supplicated for him thus, "O' Allāh ﷺ, fill him with knowledge."

He had much love and a deep relationship with the Holy Prophet ﷺ. Once, he came to learn of a person in Basra who greatly resembled the Holy Prophet ﷺ. He sent a message to the governor of Basra, to immediately send the person to him with utmost dignity and honour. When the person arrived, Sayyidunā Mu'āwiya personally advanced to welcome him and showered him with gifts and a robe of honour.

Due to the same love for the Holy Prophet ﷺ, he preserved some of his cut nails, his cloth and some hair, regarding which he bequested to be placed in his nose, ears and eyes and be buried with him. He also paid a large sum for the sheet which the Holy Prophet ﷺ gifted to Sayyidunā Ka'b Ibn Zuhair, after hearing some couplets from him.

Due to this relationship with the Holy Prophet 🌙, many of his ways bore a striking resemblance of the manners of the Holy Prophet 🌙. Sayyidunā Abū Darda ⚛ says, "I have not found anyone's Salāh so similar to the Holy Prophet's 🌙 Salāh than that of Mu'āwiya's."

Sayyidunā Jabala Ibn Suhaim ⚛ narrates, "Once, during the Khilāfat of Mu'āwiya ⚛, I came into his presence and noticed that there was a rope around his neck, which a child was pulling, with whom the Khalīfah was playing. I enquired, 'O' Amīrul Muminīn! What on earth are you doing?' He replied, 'Be quiet you silly man! I have heard the Holy Prophet 🌙 say, "Whoever has children should behave like a child to make them happy."'

Sayyidunā Mu'āwiya ⚛ prepared the first naval fleet in Muslim history and set sail for Qubrus, on 27AH with a group of Sahābah ⚛. This was the first naval expedition in Islamic history. The renowned historian Ibn Khaldūn ⚛ writes, "Sayyidunā Mu'āwiya ⚛ was the first Khalīfah who had a naval fleet prepared and through him, the Muslims got permission for a naval Jihād."

In relation to this, Imām Bukhāri ⚛ has recorded the Hadīth of the Holy Prophet 🌙, wherein he said, "The first army of my Ummah to engage in a battle at sea, will make Jannah compulsory upon themselves."

This fact can be ascertained from the faith-kindling letter which Sayyidunā Mu'āwiya ⚛ wrote to the Kaiser of Rome, during the very period of this dispute. Kaiser, noticing the winds of war blowing, decided to snatch the opportunity to initiate some military manoeuvres along the borders of Shām. Sayyidunā Mu'āwiya ⚛ received news of this and dispatched a letter to Kaiser saying, "I have received intelligence of your intentions to mobilise your forces at our borders. Take heed! If you do so, I will immediately make peace with my Companion, Sayyidunā Ali ﷺ and our ensuing army which will march inclusive of me in the first regiment, will turn Constantinople into a smouldering charcoal!" When this letter reached Kaiser, he immediately took heed and terminated all military activities. He knew very well that these people confronted disbelief as one body and soul and that their differences were unlike those of political leaders.

In this age of trial and tribulation, our Divine and pristine religion Islām is being attacked from all sides. Unfortunately, on the academic front, some unwary Muslims by name have made it their passion to speak ill, find fault, severely criticise, attack and deny the services of the Sahābah ﷺ. Those who do this concoct history, fabricate stories, misrepresent events and rely on Shia narrations to promote their evil ideas. Amongst the Sahābah ﷺ, Sayyidunā Mu'āwiya ﷺ has been the target of criticism. By questioning the integrity and honour of Sayyidunā Mu'āwiya ﷺ, one directly places the reliability and authenticity of the Holy Qur'ān in jeopardy. As a rule, stay away from one who speaks ill of Sayyidunā Mu'āwiya ﷺ, avoid one who criticises Sayyidunā Mu'āwiya ﷺ and shun the one who talks bad of Sayyidunā Mu'āwiya ﷺ. Know that the one who wilfully and intentionally criticises Sayyidunā Mu'āwiya ﷺ is not from the Ahlus Sunnat Wal Jamā'at.

Other titles from JKN Publications

Your Questions Answered

An outstanding book written by Shaykh Mufti Saiful Islām. A very comprehensive yet simple Fatāwa book and a source of guidance that reaches out to a wider audience i.e. the English speaking Muslims. The reader will benefit from the various answers to questions based on the Laws of Islām relating to the beliefs of Islām, knowledge, Sunnah, pillars of Islām, marriage, divorce and contemporary issues.

UK RRP: £7.50

Hadeeth for Beginners

A concise Hadeeth book with various Ahādeeth that relate to basic Ibādāh and moral etiquettes in Islām accessible to a wider readership. Each Hadeeth has been presented with the Arabic text, its translation and commentary to enlighten the reader, its meaning and application in day-to-day life.

UK RRP: £3.00

Du'ā for Beginners

This book contains basic Du'ās which every Muslim should recite on a daily basis. Highly recommended to young children and adults studying at Islamic schools and Madrasahs so that one may cherish the beautiful treasure of supplications of our beloved Prophet ﷺ in one's daily life, which will ultimately bring peace and happiness in both worlds, Inshā-Allāh.

UK RRP: £2.00

How well do you know Islām?

An exciting educational book which contains 300 multiple questions and answers to help you increase your knowledge on Islām! Ideal for the whole family, especially children and adult students to learn new knowledge in an enjoyable way and cherish the treasures of knowledge that you will acquire from this book. A very beneficial tool for educational syllabus.

UK RRP: £3.00

Treasures of the Holy Qur'ān

This book entitled "Treasures of the Holy Qur'ān" has been compiled to create a stronger bond between the Holy Qur'ān and the readers. It mentions the different virtues of Sūrahs and verses from the Holy Qur'ān with the hope that the readers will increase their zeal and enthusiasm to recite and inculcate the teachings of the Holy Qur'ān into their daily lives.

UK RRP: £3.00

Marriage - A Complete Solution

Islām regards marriage as a great act of worship. This book has been designed to provide the fundamental teachings and guidelines of all what relates to the marital life in a simplified English language. It encapsulates in a nutshell all the marriage laws mentioned in many of the main reference books in order to facilitate their understanding and implementation.

UK RRP: £5.00

Pearls of Luqmān

This book is a comprehensive commentary of Sūrah Luqmān, written beautifully by Shaykh Mufti Saiful Islām. It offers the reader with an enquiring mind, abundance of advice, guidance, counselling and wisdom.

The reader will be enlightened by many wonderful topics and anecdotes mentioned in this book, which will create a greater understanding of the Holy Qur'ān and its wisdom. The book highlights some of the wise sayings and words of advice Luqmān ﷺ gave to his son.

UK RRP: £3.00

Arabic Grammar for Beginners

This book is a study of Arabic Grammar based on the subject of Nahw (Syntax) in a simplified English format. If a student studies this book thoroughly, he/she will develop a very good foundation in this field, Inshā-Allāh. Many books have been written on this subject in various languages such as Arabic, Persian and Urdu. However, in this day and age there is a growing demand for this subject to be available in English .

UK RRP: £3.00

A Gift to My Youngsters

This treasure filled book, is a collection of Islamic stories, morals and anecdotes from the life of our beloved Prophet ﷺ, his Companions ﷺ and the pious predecessors. The stories and anecdotes are based on moral and ethical values, which the reader will enjoy sharing with their peers, friends, families and loved ones.

"A Gift to My Youngsters" – is a wonderful gift presented to the readers personally, by the author himself, especially with the youngsters in mind. He has carefully selected stories and anecdotes containing beautiful morals, lessons and valuable knowledge and wisdom.

UK RRP: £5.00

Travel Companion

The beauty of this book is that it enables a person on any journey, small or distant or simply at home, to utilise their spare time to read and benefit from an exciting and vast collection of important and interesting Islamic topics and lessons. Written in simple and easy to read text, this book will immensely benefit both the newly interested person in Islām and the inquiring mind of a student expanding upon their existing knowledge. Inspiring reminders from the Holy Qur'ān and the blessed words of our beloved Prophet ﷺ beautifies each topic and will illuminate the heart of the reader.   **UK RRP: £5.00**

Pearls of Wisdom

Junaid Baghdādi ﷺ once said, "Allāh ﷻ strengthens through these Islamic stories the hearts of His friends, as proven from the Qur'anic verse,
"And all that We narrate unto you of the stories of the Messengers, so as to strengthen through it your heart." (11:120)
Mālik Ibn Dinār ﷺ stated that such stories are gifts from Paradise. He also emphasised to narrate these stories as much as possible as they are gems and it is possible that an individual might find a truly rare and invaluable gem among them.   **UK RRP: £6.00**

Inspirations

This book contains a compilation of selected speeches delivered by Shaykh Mufti Saiful Islām on a variety of topics such as the Holy Qur'ān, Nikāh and eating Halāl. Having previously been compiled in separate booklets, it was decided that the transcripts be gathered together in one book for the benefit of the reader. In addition to this, we have included in this book, further speeches which have not yet been printed.

UK RRP: £6.00

Gift to my Sisters

A thought provoking compilation of very interesting articles including real life stories of pious predecessors, imaginative illustrations and much more. All designed to influence and motivate mothers, sisters, wives and daughters towards an ideal Islamic lifestyle. A lifestyle referred to by our Creator, Allāh ﷻ in the Holy Qur'ān as the means to salvation and ultimate success.

UK RRP: £6.00

Gift to my Brothers

A thought provoking compilation of very interesting articles including real life stories of pious predecessors, imaginative illustrations, medical advices on intoxicants and rehabilitation and much more. All designed to influence and motivate fathers, brothers, husbands and sons towards an ideal Islamic lifestyle. A lifestyle referred to by our Creator, Allāh ﷻ in the Holy Qur'ān as the means to salvation and ultimate success.

UK RRP: £5.00

Heroes of Islām

"In the narratives there is certainly a lesson for people of intelligence (understanding)." (12:111)

A fine blend of Islamic personalities who have been recognised for leaving a lasting mark in the hearts and minds of people.

A distinguishing feature of this book is that the author has selected not only some of the most world and historically famous renowned scholars but also these lesser known and a few who have simply left behind a valuable piece of advice to their nearest and dearest.   **UK RRP: £5.00**

Ask a Mufti (3 volumes)

Muslims in every generation have confronted different kinds of challenges. In-spite of that, Islām produced such luminary Ulamā who confronted and re-sponded to the challenges of their time to guide the Ummah to the straight path. "Ask A Mufti" is a comprehensive three volume fatwa book, based on the Hanafi School, covering a wide range of topics related to every aspect of human life such as belief, ritual worship, life after death and contemporary legal topics related to purity, commercial transaction, marriage, divorce, food, cosmetic, laws pertaining to women, Islamic medical ethics and much more.

UK RRP: £30.00

Should I Follow a Madhab?

Taqleed or following one of the four legal schools is not a new phenomenon. Historically, scholars of great calibre and luminaries, each one being a specialist in his own right, were known to have adhered to one of the four legal schools. It is only in the previous century that a minority group emerged advocating a se-vere ban on following one of the four major schools.

This book endeavours to address the topic of Taqleed and elucidates its im-portance and necessity in this day and age. It will also, by the Divine Will of Allāh ﷻ dispel some of the confusion surrounding this topic.   **UK RRP: £5.00**

Advice for the Students of Knowledge

Allāh ﷻ describes divine knowledge in the Holy Qur'ān as a 'Light'. Amongst the qualities of light are purity and guidance. The Holy Prophet ﷺ has clearly ex-plained this concept in many blessed Ahādeeth and has also taught us many supplications in which we ask for beneficial knowledge.

This book is a golden tool for every sincere student of knowledge wishing to mould his/her character and engrain those correct qualities in order to be wor-thy of receiving the great gift of Ilm from Allāh ﷻ.   **UK RRP: £3.00**

Stories for Children

"Stories for Children" - is a wonderful gift presented to the readers personally by the author himself, especially with the young children in mind. The stories are based on moral and ethical values, which the reader will enjoy sharing with their peers, friends, families and loved ones. The aim is to present to the children stories and incidents which contain moral lessons, in order to reform and correct their lives, according to the Holy Qur'ān and Sunnah.

UK RRP: £5.00

Pearls from My Shaykh

This book contains a collection of pearls and inspirational accounts of the Holy Prophet ﷺ, his noble Companions, pious predecessors and some personal accounts and sayings of our well-known contemporary scholar and spiritual guide, Shaykh Mufti Saiful Islām Sāhib. Each anecdote and narrative of the pious predecessors have been written in the way that was narrated by Mufti Saiful Islām Sāhib in his discourses, drawing the specific lessons he intended by telling the story. The accounts from the life of the Shaykh has been compiled by a particular student based on their own experience and personal observation. **UK RRP: £5.00**

Paradise & Hell

This book is a collection of detailed explanation of Paradise and Hell including the state and conditions of its inhabitants. All the details have been taken from various reliable sources. The purpose of its compilation is for the reader to contemplate and appreciate the innumerable favours, rewards, comfort and unlimited luxuries of Paradise and at the same time take heed from the punishment of Hell. Shaykh Mufti Saiful Islām Sāhib has presented this book in a unique format by including the Tafseer and virtues of Sūrah Ar-Rahmān. **UK RRP: £5.00**

Prayers for Forgiveness

Prayers for Forgiveness' is a short compilation of Du'ās in Arabic with English translation and transliteration. This book can be studied after 'Du'ā for Beginners' or as a separate book. It includes twenty more Du'ās which have not been mentioned in the previous Du'ā book. It also includes a section of Du'ās from the Holy Qur'ān and a section from the Ahādeeth. The book concludes with a section mentioning the Ninety-Nine Names of Allāh ﷻ with its translation and transliteration. **UK RRP: £3.00**

Scattered Pearls

This book is a collection of scattered pearls taken from books, magazines, emails and WhatsApp messages. These pearls will hopefully increase our knowledge, wisdom and make us realise the purpose of life. In this book, Mufti Sāhib has included messages sent to him from scholars, friends and colleagues which will be beneficial and interesting for our readers Inshā-Allāh. **UK RRP: £4.00**

Poems of Wisdom

This book is a collection of poems from those who contributed to the Al-Mumin Magazine in the poems section. The Hadeeth mentions "Indeed some form of poems are full of wisdom." The themes of each poem vary between wittiness, thought provocation, moral lessons, emotional to name but a few. The readers will benefit from this immensely and make them ponder over the outlook of life in general.

UK RRP: £4.00

Horrors of Judgement Day

This book is a detailed and informative commentary of the first three Sūrahs of the last Juz namely; Sūrah Naba, Sūrah Nāzi'āt and Sūrah Abasa. These Sūrahs vividly depict the horrific events and scenes of the Great Day in order to warn mankind the end of this world. These Sūrahs are an essential reminder for us all to instil the fear and concern of the Day of Judgement and to detach ourselves from the worldly pleasures. Reading this book allows us to attain the true realization of this world and provides essential advices of how to gain eternal salvation in the Hereafter.

RRP: £5:00

Spiritual Heart

It is necessary that Muslims always strive to better themselves at all times and to free themselves from the destructive maladies. This book focusses on three main spiritual maladies; pride, anger and evil gazes. It explains its root causes and offers some spiritual cures. Many examples from the lives of the pious predecessors are used for inspiration and encouragement for controlling the above three maladies. It is hoped that the purification process of the heart becomes easy once the underlying roots of the above maladies are clearly understood.   **UK RRP: £5:00**

Hajj & Umrah for Beginners

This book is a step by step guide on Hajj and Umrah for absolute beginners. Many other additional important rulings (Masāil) have been included that will Insha-Allāh prove very useful for our readers. The book also includes some etiquettes of visiting (Ziyārat) of the Holy Prophet's ﷺ blessed Masjid and his Holy Grave.

UK RRP £3:00

Advice for the Spiritual Travellers

This book contains essential guidelines for a spiritual Murīd to gain some familiarity of the science of Tasawwuf. It explains the meaning and aims of Tasawwuf, some understanding around the concept of the soul, and general guidelines for a spiritual Murīd. This is highly recommended book and it is hoped that it gains wider readership among those Murīds who are basically new to the science of Tasawwuf.

UK RRP £3:00

Don't Worry Be Happy

This book is a compilation of sayings and earnest pieces of advice that have been gathered directly from my respected teacher Shaykh Mufti Saiful Islām Sāhib. The book consists of many valuable enlightenments including how to deal with challenges of life, promoting unity, practicing good manners, being optimistic and many other valuable advices. Our respected Shaykh has gathered this Naseehah from meditating, contemplating, analysing and searching for the gems within Qur'anic verses, Ahādeeth and teachings of our Pious Predecessors. **UK RRP £1:00**

Kanzul Bāri

Kanzul Bāri provides a detailed commentary of the Ahādeeth contained in Saheeh al-Bukhāri. The commentary includes Imām Bukhāri's ﷺ biography, the status of his book, spiritual advice, inspirational accounts along with academic discussions related to Fiqh, its application and differences of opinion. Moreover, it answers objections arising in one's mind about certain Ahādeeth. Inquisitive students of Hadeeth will find this commentary a very useful reference book in the final year of their Ālim course for gaining a deeper understanding of the science of Hadeeth. **UK RRP: £15.00**

How to Become a Friend of Allāh ﷺ

The friends of Allāh ﷺ have been described in detail in the Holy Qur'ān and Āhadeeth. This book endeavours its readers to help create a bond with Allāh ﷺ in attaining His friendship as He is the sole Creator of all material and immaterial things. It is only through Allāh's ﷺ friendship, an individual will achieve happiness in this life and the Hereafter, hence eliminate worries, sadness, depression, anxiety and misery of this world. **UK RRP: £3.00**

Gems & Jewels

This book contains a selection of articles which have been gathered for the benefit of the readers covering a variety of topics on various aspects of daily life. It offers precious advice and anecdotes that contain moral lessons. The advice captivates its readers and will extend the narrowness of their thoughts to deep reflection, wisdom and appreciation of the purpose of our existence. **UK RRP: £4.00**

End of Time

This book is a comprehensive explanation of the three Sūrahs of Juzz Amma; Sūrah Takweer, Sūrah Infitār and Sūrah Mutaffifeen. This book is a continuation from the previous book of the same author, 'Horrors of Judgement Day'. The three Sūrahs vividly sketch out the scene of the Day of Judgement and describe the state of both the inmates of Jannah and Jahannam. Mufti Saiful Islām Sāhib provides an easy but comprehensive commentary of the three Sūrahs facilitating its understanding for the readers whilst capturing the horrific scene of the ending of the world and the conditions of mankind on that horrific Day. **UK RRP: £5.00**

Ideal Youth
This book contains articles gathered from various social media avenues; magazines, emails, WhatsApp and telegram messages that provide useful tips of advice for those who have the zeal to learn and consider changing their negative habits and behavior and become better Muslims to set a positive trend for the next generation. **UK RRP:£4:00**

Ideal Teacher
This book contains abundance of precious advices for the Ulamā who are in the teaching profession. It serves to present Islamic ethical principles of teaching and to remind every teacher of their moral duties towards their students. This book will Inshā-Allāh prove to be beneficial for newly graduates and scholars wanting to utilize their knowledge through teaching. **UK RRP:£4:00**

Ideal Student
This book is a guide for all students of knowledge in achieving the excellent qualities of becoming an ideal student. It contains precious advices, anecdotes of our pious predecessors and tips in developing good morals as a student. Good morals is vital for seeking knowledge. A must for all students if they want to develop their Islamic Knowledge. **UK RRP:£4:00**

Andalus (modern day Spain), the long lost history, was once a country that produced many great calibre of Muslim scholars comprising of Mufassirūn, Muhaddithūn, Fuqahā, judges, scientists, philosophers, surgeons, to name but a few. The Muslims conquered Andalus in 711 AD and ruled over it for eight-hundred years. This was known as the era of Muslim glory. Many non-Muslim Europeans during that time travelled to Spain to study under Muslim scholars. The remanences of the Muslim rule in Spain are manifested through their universities, magnificent palaces and Masājid carved with Arabic writings, standing even until today. In this book, Shaykh Mufti Saiful Islām shares some of his valuable experiences he witnessed during his journey to Spain. **UK RRP: £3.00**